Spirituality- Unlocking the Mystery

8 Keys to Self Fulfillment

> Pssst!
>
> Check this out!
> Spirituality
> 101

**By
David Sides**

INFINITE INSIGHTS
Publishing

Spirituality-Unlocking the Mystery
Copyright © 2002
By Infinite Insights Publishing

Cover design by Frank Sierra
      Nature's Artistry
Photo of Author by Doreen Wynja
      Eye of the Lady Photography

All rights reserved. No part of this book may be reproduced or transmitted in any form or by any means electronic or mechanical, including photocopying, recording, or by any information storage retrieval system, except in brief quotation with proper credit given, without permission in writing from the publisher and/or author himself.

ISBN: 0-9741146-0-X
Library of Congress Catalog Number: 1-055-576

Library of Congress Cataloging-in-Publication Data
Under previous title of: Unlocking the Spiritual Laws of the Universe
                By David Sides

Infinite Insights Publishing
PO Box 230056
Tigard, OR 97281

Printed in the United States

There are only three
choices in life:
The Past
    The Present
        The Future

You decide in
which to live.

Situations happened
Yesterday
Promises Happen
Tomorrow
Life happens
NOW!

David Sides

Much Love & Mercy Marie
Blessings
David Sides

Dedication

I dedicate this book to Amy Farmer.
When I met you Amy, I met myself.
I came to know the *"essence"* of Love.
I came to know the *"essence"* of Life itself.
I came to know clarity like I have never known.
You are the reason I have lived my life this long.
Through you, I came to know that I am the
Love I choose to share in this world.
I will *never* forget you Amy.
I will *always* Love you.
Thank you.

Table of Contents

Acknowledgements..ii

Preface..vi

Chapter One
The Keys to Thinking Thought..........................1

Chapter Two
The Keys to Attraction.......................................13

Chapter Three
The Keys to Giving & Receiving.......................27

Chapter Four
The Keys to Detachment...................................39

Chapter Five
The Keys to Gratitude..53

Chapter Six
The Keys to Love (Subtitled: The Keys to Increase)......67

Chapter Seven
The Keys to Forgiveness...................................79

Chapter Eight
The Keys to Faith...97

In Conclusion...108

Your Journey Begins Here................................116

About the Author..120

©2002

Acknowledgments

As we move along through this journey called life, there will always be someone there to help us. If ever we think that we can do it alone, then we are missing a big part of our life. It is with tremendous gratitude that I acknowledge *all* of the people who have come and gone in my life. Without them taking even the smallest amount of time to assist me on my path, I would not be who I am or where I am today.

I have an enormous amount of gratitude for my circle of friends in Longview, Washington, all of who pulled me into their loving presence and nurtured my soul. The strength, wisdom, and knowledge of the reality that we *are* spiritual beings having a human experience began with you. I will always be grateful to you for showering me with the truth.

My gratitude flows deep for this spiritual family currently in my life. You have accepted me for who I am and invited me to be a part of a community that has changed my life. I acknowledge each one of you for the compassion and support you have shown me without question.

It is with gratitude that I thank Tom & Karen Hanzlik for their friendship and support. Thank you Karen for inviting me to be a part of an awesome organization that is changing the way our kids approach life. I look forward to continued friendship and partnership with both of you.

Ruth Smith and Howard Busse, thank you for opening your hearts and your home to me at a time of great transition. Ruth, there are not enough words to express the depth of my gratitude to you for remaining my friend. Because you visualized and knew this is where I would flourish, I am eternally grateful. The value of your insight is of the highest caliber.   I Thank You

Mark Olmstead, thank you for staying by my side at a time of tremendous pain. Because of your desire to see my pain pass, I experienced the calm between the Light and the Dark. I am deeply grateful for your willingness to be a part of the greater good for this work with your music.

I would like to give thanks to Deanna Forseth for inviting me into her home and giving me a safe place to rebuild my life at a time of great difficulty.

I would like to give special thanks to Frank Sierra for taking my concept for the cover of this book to a new level. Frank, you really expressed my heart through your creative genius. Thank you!

I am grateful for Michael Walker for taking the time to create my website.

I am grateful and appreciate the coaches of Lifeline Coaching & Education, especially Steve & Lynn Wiltshire. You both have touched my life. You are an example to live by. Melissa Schenk, I want to thank you for your kind friendship. You are one of a kind. Thank you for befriending me. I will always be grateful for you.

There are two people in my life now I have met recently that have supported me without knowing me, and for this I will continue to hold them in my heart. Anthony and Renee' Choice separately you are very powerful individuals, but as a couple you are like the lighthouse and the light. One cannot work without the other.

I support you both to shine on and guide as many souls as you can to a safe port. Thank you both for coaxing my greatness to the surface. Without you the launch would not have been as successful.

I would also like to acknowledge all of you who are or have been involved in the **Living Enrichment Circles.** Your kindness allows others to grow at their own pace, and this has quickened my pace.

Most importantly, Reverend Mary Manin Morrissey, I will always carry in my heart that for which you came to this world. I cannot reach deep enough to share with you how you have impacted my life. The compassionate wisdom you share greatly enhances my life, as well as many others, and we will never be the same. Thank God. I am so grateful that we share this life at the same time. I cannot find enough words or expressions to share about being invited into your family. I will always be there for you, anytime and for any reason, just ask.

Jack and Dorothy Manin. (A.K.A. Mom and Dad) Thank you both for sharing your gifts with me. I will be forever grateful for your kindness and generosity. I am blessed to know you. Rest in peace Mr. Jack.

The wonderful staff and volunteers at **Living Enrichment Center,** thank you all for the work you have put into building a community for those who desire a deeper, more meaningful relationship with community and God.

I give gratitude for my family-mostly, my mother and father. Without them, I would not be here to find my way back to God.

It was in that journey, all of it, that I have become the man I am today. Thank you for your patience with me, and thank you for bringing me into this world.

Mostly, I would like to show my highest gratitude to God. Getting to know you God has been one of the most difficult, enlightening and rewarding journeys I have ever embarked upon. In gathering the knowledge of who you are, I have come to know myself at a greater level than I ever thought possible. Thank you for the wisdom and the words for this book. I am grateful to know "how" you really exist in our lives. I am equally excited to finish out this life with you working in and through me *and* at my side.

Thank You God!

Preface

As you begin this book keep in mind:
"The wise man changes his mind, the fool, never."
Raymond Holliwell.

I encourage and support you in keeping an open mind. Those of you who set in motion a new way of looking at your world can make the changes you desire and live the life you truly envision for yourself and those you truly love.

Life is about perceptions. How and when you perceive something is the direction your life will take-be it negative or positive. If you perceive a situation as bad, that is exactly what it is. However, if you see the good, any good in that same situation, then you have made a shift in your perception that changes your life, for the better.

In that shift of seeing life's situations differently, you have unlocked one door and you begin to open your world to the wonderful gifts of abundance. Please keep in mind that abundance comes in many forms. Money is only one form of the countless ways that abundance shows up in our lives.

One such way is food. Think about it for a moment. Are you thankful for the food you receive regardless of what or how much? If not, express gratitude for the next meal and experience what happens. If you are not sure where to send that thankfulness, close your eyes and think of the whole Universe and just say, "thank you." This will be covered more in the chapter entitled the Keys to Gratitude.

My goal in this book is to share with you knowledge that has been with us for thousands of years.

Jesus studied these spiritual principles and knew how they worked in his life. That is what he came to teach us. That is what made his teachings so profound. He understood and lived these principles. He gathered and used the keys that unlocked the principles that will lead us all to our highest good.

It is my privilege to show you how to tap into your creative power through this knowledge. Once you are aware of how to bring forth your powers according to Spiritual Laws and understand that *your thoughts do determine your destiny,* it is *your responsibility* to apply them in a way that brings forth your desired destiny.

Wouldn't you rather live the life you've seen in your minds eye - the life where *you choose* how to live? If you continue to think less than impeccable thoughts, it will be very difficult to move your life in the direction you desire.
I will not pretend this is easy. We've lived a long time with some of our habits. As you obtain the keys that unlock the spiritual principles and understand how they work in your life, there will be some disruptions of those habits. You've heard the phrase, "Old habits die hard?" As you already know, some of them will hang on and put up a fight. You won't get rid of them overnight. You will, however, transform them if you work with these spiritual principles and allow new ways of thinking to begin. As your new thoughts emerge, your old habits will have difficulty finding ways of expression.

I do want to *caution you* about what will take place in your life when you begin to practice positive changes.

There will always be those in your life, family as well as friends, who will notice "a change" in you and will feel threatened that in your growth, they will get left behind. First of all, the ones that do not support you in your growth are the ones that have been holding you back. Let them know it is time for you to move forward with your life. Tell them you care and move on anyway. If they are supportive, invite them to come along in their growth. Share with them the keys you have obtained and show them how to unlock these principles for their life. Build a small group of those friends who want to see each other succeed and will support each other in growing toward that success. Have each of them get a copy of this book so all of you can work together and assist each other in understanding these laws, these spiritual principles. It is in understanding these basic spiritual principles that you obtain the keys to fulfillment in your life.

One last thing before you embark upon a new way of life. There *is* a power in this universe that is greater than you or I. It is a power we can call upon at any time. It is in the acknowledgement of this power that allows a greater understanding of these spiritual principles to emerge. This power has been called Divine Intelligence, Spiritual Mind, God, Spirit, Love, Light and numerous other names. I am not here to challenge your beliefs or what you choose to call this power. Only to let you know that whatever your beliefs are, I honor and respect them. I would encourage you to use the name that comforts you the most.

These spiritual principles do not have a preference on what you call them.

If you do not have a belief in anything other than the power within you then call it that, i.e., I give thanks to the power within me. It is a power that is all around and permeates all living things. So why would this power *not* be within you? When you look for it, you will find it.

It is my sincere hope that you will magnetize all the good that you desire and that all your dreams are fulfilled.

Keep this in mind as you begin your journey:

"A mystery only remains a mystery when ignorance and unbelief exist. There is no mystery where there is knowledge and faith."

Alice A. Bailey

Enjoy your journey.

I HAVE LOST FRIENDS, SOME BY DEATH —
OTHERS THROUGH THE SHEER *INABILITY*
TO CROSS THE STREET.

VIRGINIA WOOLF

Chapter One

The Keys to Thinking & Thought

In sharing this ancient knowledge with you there is an ending-taking place in my personal life. It is not only one of relationship, but also the loss of my job. I tell you this since the ending of one part of life, is a perfect place to start anew.

It is a real challenge to keep my thoughts from going astray. It is in times like these that we tend to be hard on ourselves. Some of our first thoughts are to blame the circumstances around us. We want to blame ourselves for what we didn't do or what we should have done or could have done better. We *think* about all the reasons why we do not deserve what we wanted to include in our lives. It is in believing those reasons and *that* thinking; *we* end up creating the turmoil in our lives. Let me explain.

We know we have within us the ability to obtain anything we want. We start out doing the things that have long been a desire inside. We feel that desire welling up inside and all of the sudden, we are off and running toward that new dream. Then, after a short period of time we seem to run out of energy on the way to what we imagined to be a better life. What happens? What stops us?

It is *our own thoughts* that seemingly bring life to a halt. In reality life does not come to a halt. It only changes direction much like your car changes direction when you turn one way or another. When we think about changing direction in our life, we invite that thought to reach into the universe and find whatever we are thinking about.

My life changed direction because I invited it, through thought, to do so. One week before I was fired I had the thought, "Don't get comfortable here because if you stay, your dreams won't come true." The universe responded to my thoughts about the job. When the universe finds what we ask for, it responds and brings to us the manifestation of those thoughts we are holding onto. Sometimes it happens so quickly, we call it a miracle-or curse depending on what we have brought into our lives. At times it may take a little longer depending on the amount of time and energy put into that thought. You make it happen as fast or as slowly as you choose. When you stay focused on *that which you desire*, there's an immediate shift in the energy we are all a part of. To bring forth the desired results can be complex. However, the more we stay connected to and work within these spiritual laws, we can manifest our dreams very quickly, as compared to the length of time we have on this earth.

If you ever were curious how fast our thoughts travel, here's a piece of science trivia for you. In <u>Working With The Law</u> Raymond Holliwell indicates that our thoughts travel at the same speed light travels. If thoughts *are* energy then they may travel faster than light.

> Light travels at 186,000 miles per second. That is 930,000 times faster than your voice or the speed of sound.

It is believed that a thought, your thought, can travel around the world from pole to pole many times in less than a second.

It is the only force in the universe known to humans that can travel that fast. Is it any wonder that when we approach someone we don't know, we have a sense about him or her? Did they look at you before you made eye contact and have a thought about you, and did you pick up on that thought? You have probably experienced it first hand when you think about a friend or family member, who lives hundreds or thousands of miles away, and suddenly they are calling you. That's how fast your thoughts can travel.

    Now that you know how fast our thoughts travel, wouldn't it be fair to say that what you're thinking about yourself could be what those around you are thinking, simply because you let them know *what you think* the world and universe thinks about you? Since you sent the thought out into the universe, it responded in like kind. Additionally, knowing that your thoughts could reach someone in a flash, why would you entertain any thoughts other than kind ones?

> Charles Fillmore in his book, <u>Talks On Truth</u> states, "Every act of hu-man-ity has its origin in thought, which is expressed into the world from a mental center that is but a point of radiation for an energy that lies back of it."

    In other words, when you think a thought, there is an energy that responds in bringing what you think into reality. Why would you think negative thoughts if you knew those thoughts would manifest into your reality? As previously mentioned, the thoughts we think are the most powerful force we as humans know. This force can be directed to bring about the life we truly desire. Misdirected, it can keep us from our dreams and/or destroy what we currently have in our lives. It is not unlike electricity. Misdirected, it can be very destructive in our lives, not unlike lightening when it strikes at random. Directed and controlled, electricity can be and is a wonderful addition to our lives. Our thoughts, directed and controlled, can bring about amazing results in our lives. Consider this: The thoughts you think remain thoughts until they are un-thought - in essence changing your mind about how you view what you hold in your mind. Do you continue to think about something that took place many years ago? If so, keep in mind it remains a thought until it is un-thought - until that thought is re-thought and cleared. To clear any thoughts that might be keeping you stuck, you must re-think them. When you give new and clear meaning to what you think about, new and clear ways of directing your life will appear.

      How do we direct our thoughts and our thinking? Keep in mind that we are always thinking. We are thinking machines. We cannot stop thinking. We can change our thoughts much like we change the direction of our car just by thinking about it. You may have heard about cause and effect (and you may be) aware that what you think produces some kind of effect. What kind of effect do you want to produce in your life? When you think about something does it have merit or is it just aimless thought? Are you caught up in the thoughts of your habits and conditioning? If so, this is where we need to consciously design what we think, especially about ourselves. How do we change the thinking that has conditioned us to a worst-case scenario of neutral and a best-case scenario of creating our dreams?

First, keep in mind what has conditioned you is a combination of those authority figures you grew up with and may not necessarily reflect your own personal thoughts and beliefs about who you really are. Really look at that. Is what you believe *your beliefs* or someone else's?

Secondly, remember the quote by Albert Einstein; "The significant problems we face cannot be solved at the level of thinking that created them." In other words, if you want to move past your current lifestyle or lack thereof, you must move to the next level of thinking. What is the next level of thinking and how do we move into it?

In order to move to the next level of thinking, we must increase our awareness of who we really are, what we want and what we think about. By becoming aware of what we think about on a daily basis we can sift through those unconscious thoughts and/or habits that surface to our conscious mind. Once those unwanted habits arise to a conscious level, to our awareness, we can change them, producing better results.

Think of the following diagram as our mind. What comes from our unconscious mind flows into our conscious mind, there by producing our results.

```
    Unconscious
           Mind
    ─────────────
    Conscious Mind
    ─────────────
        Results
```

What is consciousness? It is described as the sum total of our inner awareness. If it is true what we hold in our consciousness is all that we are aware of, and from there create all things, then why would we ignore the steps it takes to create a larger awareness? In creating that larger awareness *"we can"* obtain all of our desires. The following story is an illustration of one level of awareness.

Have you ever heard the story of the man who was looking around a train yard one day and came across an old refrigerator car and decided to explore the inside? As he went inside to look around the door closed and latched behind him. He pounded and shouted for a few minutes in an attempt to get someone to help him out of the train car. No one heard his cries for help. His thoughts then shifted to the possibility that he could freeze to death since he was in a refrigerated car. Inside he scratched onto the walls what his last moments were like. He wrote/scratched how he was feeling numb and cold. At one point he wrote what were considered to be his last thoughts. The man died in the train refrigerator car. He was found in a frozen state. The authorities were puzzled and could not determine how this man became frozen, since freezing is 32 degrees. Upon discovering the refrigerator unit in the train car was malfunctioning, the authorities checked the temperature and learned that it had not dropped below 40 degrees, which added to their bewilderment.

Why tell this story? To show you the power of the mind. The powers of our thoughts are such that this man thought himself to death.

If our thoughts are powerful enough to talk us into death, are they not equally powerful enough to end our struggles with money and happiness?

We can end our struggles by choosing a new way of thinking about them. Think about your trials as the part of life you've chosen to explore and now no longer chose to explore. You must be careful here not to get caught up in thinking, "I don't want this," since *what you hold in mind reproduces in kind.* In order to change your mind, it is important to "think" about what you want instead of what you see with your physical eyes. We have been trained to think what we see with our eyes is what we get. This is not true. What you see with your physical eye is what you have been thinking.

In other words, the world you have created is a reflection of the thoughts you held in your mind. What you see in the outer world is a memory in your brain. In reality, our imagination *is* the mind's eye, so we see with the mind instead of the eye. Hold in your mind the picture of the life you truly desire. Let your imagination paint a picture of the reality you want, not what you know it to be or what you currently see. Your unconscious mind does not know the difference between a real or imagined picture. It is only delivering what you asked for.

Get a clear picture of where you are going and what you want in life. If you want to arrive at your destination you must map out where you are going. Define your destination. What does it look like when you arrive? You must also have a purpose. Why are going there? Do you know what you will do to get to that destination?

When you take an important trip you don't take off and say, "We'll figure out where we're going along the way." Because it's important, you know before you leave where you are going. You also know what places you will pass along the way. These places let you know you are still on the right path toward your predetermined destination. It is the same when you are about to embark upon a journey of becoming wealthy-in all areas of your life. You must choose the vehicle that will get you there, know which direction you will take, know which mile post you will pass, and have a time frame set in place.

As you obtain and work with The Keys of Thinking & Thought the universe responds to what you want. Please note whatever you want and ask for you shall receive, even if you have negative thoughts about it. You make the choice about what you want to receive in this world, even if you say you *don't* want something you have made a choice with that thought and the picture of what you *don't* want in your mind. (Don't think of a pink elephant). Get the picture?

Would you rather receive all the good the universe has provided for you just for thinking differently than you have in the past or do you want to stay with the life you now have by thinking the same thoughts and holding onto the same perceptions? When you think bigger and more valuable thoughts about you and the world around you, you receive greater and higher means to live the life you desire. You can attract all that you desire. One of the best ways to accomplish this is to *think* about what you really love to do, not what you believe you *have* to do.

As this chapter comes to a close I would like to leave you with a quote from Rumi, an ancient poet, and a poem I wrote long before this book came to mind.

"Think of who created thought! Why do you stay in prison when the door is wide open?"

Rumi

The Circle of Life

As a stone is cast into the water,
So too are our spirits cast into life.
The size of the stone determines
the size of the circle,
The size of our thoughts determine
how big we are in this life.

Throw a small stone into the water,
the circle is limited.
Throw a small thought into this world,
our growth is also limited.

By throwing a larger stone,
you create a larger circle.
To create a larger circle of life you must
throw bigger and better thoughts into the world.

It is by the thoughts of our own making that
determine and create our circle of life,
be it large or be it small.

Here is your Key to
thinking bigger and better thoughts
about you and your life.

Start by noticing what kind of thoughts you are having about your life, your job or career, your family and all the things that make up your life.

List out your thoughts and then notice where you could make some changes.

EX: Let's say you have a thought about your job that comes up and says my job sucks and I need to find a new job.

In order to have a new thought about this I would suggest you start by giving gratitude for what this job has done for you.

Go back to the beginning of your job and ask yourself: What have I learned from this job that has prepared me for the next job?

The new thought might go something like this: I am grateful for this job and what it has taught me. I appreciate the boss for taking the time to teach me what I have learned. I am grateful the skills I have learned have prepared me for my next job, which now comes to me in the perfect way and for the perfect pay.

Keep a journal with you and notice the thoughts that keep repeating. These are thoughts that keep you in habitual thinking which leads you to habitual living. Do you want to break the habits that keep you stuck? Break the repetition of thoughts that are holding you back by repeating the new thought often and daily until the old thought has faded away. The thought you feed the most is the thought that will continue to guide your life.

For your convenience I have included a few pages for you to use as a journal beginning on page 116.

FAITH IS DARING THE SOUL TO GO BEYOND
WHAT THE EYES CAN SEE

ANONYMOUS

Chapter Two

The Keys to Attraction

Desire and expectation. What do the two have to do with your money and, how do they work together?

The easiest example I can give you is the process of writing this book. I *desire* to share with you the knowledge that has been imparted to me, and at the same time I *expect* what I write will come to me in the way that will be easiest to understand. What do I mean by that?

Let's explore *desire* first. The word desire, according to Webster means: "to wish for or to have a strong want." The natural longing that is excited by the enjoyment or the thought of *any good* and impels to action or effort its continuance or possession; an eager wish to obtain or enjoy.

The Latin root or base meaning of De-sire is "Of the Father." In other words, when you have a desire, Divine Intelligence has already determined you are worthy of the thing desired, since the desire came from the Father, God. How does desire play a role in our lives?

The way in which desire plays a role in our lives is evident in what we feel we must obtain. I am writing this book at a time when, in the past, I would have been rather discouraged. I lost my job about a week ago, my relationship ended and I had to move, all within three days. You are probably wondering how I can write about such things with all this around me? As mentioned above, the thought of any good impels us to take action.

Since I have always wanted to share these ideas with more people, and want to take my growth to the next level, I now have the time, which is "The Good," that impels me to action-to walk my talk. In writing this, my desire for you is that you will have a greater understanding of how to attract everything you want into your life. Because of my deep desire I trust this book will be complete. It is in your desire to be, to do or to have the things that mean the most to you that will determine how well you succeed at whatever you choose to do.

I encourage you to keep in mind how the keys to thinking work as you use your desire to move into using the keys to attraction to fulfill your life.

> Wallace Wattles says in his book, <u>The Science of Getting Rich,</u> "Do not forget for a moment that the thinking substance *is* in everything, communicating *with* everything, and able *to* influence everything."

What we think about is responsible for all the things that have been created in life and will be responsible for all the creations to come.

That's some power!

The easiest way to describe how the keys to attraction and desire work together, as a lock and key work together, is to remember how you have used this power in your own life. The simplest one for most of us is when we go shopping. We have the desire to go the mall to purchase some new items. We think about which side of the mall we would like to be on while we are en-route to the chosen store. Arriving into the parking lot, a desire to park as close as possible propels us to notice a front row parking space. Do you think it was luck or a coincidence? The reason you were able to find that parking space is because you were in tune with the laws of attraction. You set an intention of where you wanted to be, turned down a particular row, one of many, and the universe was responding to your intention and directed you to what you desired. This is a fairly simple "test" if you will. I encourage you to work with something you have wanted, something small to start.

Another example is one of attracting money to us. How many times have you been in a position where something comes up in your life and you needed to raise some money quickly to take care of a circumstance? When these situations arise the first thing we generally do is begin to worry about where the money is coming from. (Please keep in mind that worry only drives away the thing desired). Let's say you need to pull together $400.00 by next Tuesday. You <u>must</u> have this amount. The intention is set and the desire is strong. We open to the possibilities for $400.00 to come to us. If you are in tune with the laws of attraction and the laws of gratitude, which we will talk about in a subsequent chapter, that $400.00 will and has shown up in your life just when you needed it.

I offer you this next thought on attracting money from a sign I read on the side of a bus while I was driving around town. I thought about putting this in chapter one since it starts with how we think. However, it also energizes how we attract money into our lives.

The sign read; "The filthy rich don't seem so filthy when you become one of them."

How many times have we either said; they are filthy rich or heard someone say it? When you think about that statement, especially the two words, "filthy rich" does that not set up a conflict within ourselves? Explanation: If you have ever thought about being financially rich and yet held the belief that being rich means being filthy then wouldn't you avoid being rich so you could stay clean? Most of us were raised to keep ourselves clean and yet if we hold this belief that money is dirty then how can we ever attract it into our lives? If being rich means being filthy then we will "wash away riches" just to stay clean.

I offer you a new thought, a new affirmation around this.

> As my body, mind and spirit are cleansed daily so to is all the money that flows to and through me. Since I am clean, the money that flows into my life is clean and as it flows out it is cleaning all the lives it touches. I am immaculately rich and squeaky clean with all my financial affairs.

From this point forward as when we speak of others with money we should not only bless them but also say; WOW, look at them, they are immaculately rich.

Changing the words we speak about money, ours or someone else's will attract it sooner into our lives.

The laws of attraction reach into many areas of our lives. For example, we have a desire to read a certain book and sometimes within hours after expressing our desire, the book shows up in our life through a variety of efforts (including our own)! –Or--we want to learn about something unfamiliar to us, and before we know it someone with the knowledge we seek or someone who can point us in the right direction appears. We think when something like this happens it is strange or as most of us have heard, a little "woo woo." The desire we have for more knowledge, more friendships or even more money is not so much about the desire for that thing or success that we want; the desire goes deeper than most of us are even aware. It is a desire to express ourselves at a deeper level. Once we understand that within each one of us is unexpressed expression, we can let go of what we think is our source (the paycheck, the employer, the investments) and move fully into bringing that expression forth. Expressing that which is inside each of us is our source of deep, true satisfaction. It is an expression of the most high, an expression of the Divine.

"Show up to express yourself rather than to find yourself."
Mary Manin Morrissey

It is now time to look at expectation and how it ties in with the desire to be, do and have all that we want. The word expectation has several meanings. However, they both have a relatively common theme.

Webster explains: The prospect of the future; grounds upon which something excellent is expected to happen; the prospect of anything good to come.

Expectation works in more ways than one. It can bring to you the things you want and the things you *do not* want. We will look at the latter first, the attraction of things not wanted.

When you hold in your mind anything long enough, you will see that which you hold beginning to show up in your life. You may ask how is this possible? It works two ways.

One is the *intention* you focus upon. When you keep in mind even the things you do not want to happen there is no way they cannot come to pass since you have put so much thought and energy into them. If you keep moving around this life thinking about the things you do not want to happen to you, that is exactly what you will get. The universe is only responding to that which you have asked for or held in the forefront of your mind. You might say "Well I didn't ask to be fired from my job." At some level of thinking we ask to be let go from that position so we could move forward in our lives, to claim the greater good waiting for us. An example of accepting responsibility of thought is when, after thinking about becoming an artist over and over again, you manifest that reality-with practice. Since you essentially told the universe what you wanted, it responded in like kind, gave you a key and you were let go from your job whether you thought you were ready or not. The universe wants for you what you want for yourself.

If you have had major changes in your life such as losing a job or maybe a relationship ending, it is something you asked for on a divine or Spiritual level for your continued growth and evolvement. Please keep in mind I am not stating that you are responsible for the more tragic things in life. However, there is always good to be found from these situations in our lives as well. It is up to us to *look* for the good.

The second way is one of *verbal attraction.* I've studied Neuro-Linguistic Programming (NLP) from Bennett/Stellar University in Seattle, WA. Over 30 years of study have been made in the area of language. The use of language and how what we say and hear over and over again can and will program us. In addition to being programmed by what is being said and heard, the unconscious mind does not recognize negatives or negative words. e.g.: If you state that you want to see your parents for the weekend it is pretty likely you will see them. However, If you state, "I don't want to see my parents this weekend," and that statement is one of conviction, it is still pretty likely you will see them. Why? All the unconscious mind heard is the same statement. The unconscious mind did not recognize the "don't" in your statement. Even though you did not make an attempt to see them, they picked up on your thoughts of wanting to see them. (Remember, thought travels faster than the speed of light.)

The same holds true for what you *want* in your life. If you think about what you want instead of what you don't want, you will receive that as well. The quickest way of getting what you desire in life is to believe that it is already here and state it in the positive. Someone else has already obtained everything you could ever want. All that you have ever wanted *is* available to you as well. By stating what you want in the positive you are telling the universe this is the thing desired.

One of the best ways I am sure you have already heard about is "positive affirmations."

When you say the same thing over and over again you imprint it upon your unconscious mind, which tends to be the captain of our ship. Once the desire and beliefs are imprinted through repetition, the captain of your ship, your unconscious mind, will begin navigating according to the new charts you have drawn out.

> Try this affirmation. I admit it might not be for all of us, but I would like you to be open and just say this once every day for a month.

> The Divine Consciousness that I am is forever expressing its true nature of abundance through me.

In the repetition of such statements and affirmations your unconscious mind will begin to know you are *that* person and begin looking for the fulfillment of your statements. Your job is to believe it-even if your body and mind see it differently. You must *believe* you can have all your desires in order to manifest them.

This is where expectation comes in. Once you make known your desires to the Universe, and follow the Spiritual Laws by thinking bigger and better thoughts and telling the Universe, that Divine Intelligence, what you want, it is now time to have the expectation that you will receive the object of your desire. Expect that it will come to you. Act as if you have already received your desired good-adopt an *attitude of gratitude* for what you know is coming. When you do this you are telling the universe you believe you can have all you want. When the universe hears and knows you believe it, there is *no way* you will not receive it.

I would like to awaken you to another possibility to obtaining the keys to attraction.

After you set your intention and desire toward that which you want and show your expectation to the universe, add this little phrase to your verbal and written desires: *This or something better.* It is important for you to be aware of this, since what we ask for sometimes shows up as something different or better than we expected. If we know we will receive that which we ask for or something better, then all we have to do is give gratitude in advance and act as if what we want is already here.

> Raymond Holliwell in his book, Working With the Law, says this of desire and expectation: Desire embraces a positive process of attraction; that is, when an individual earnestly desires a thing he sets up a line of force that connects him with the good desired. Expectation is an active form of attention; it is attention with intensity. Desire connects you to the thing desired and expectation draws it into your life.

I would like to add that when you are working with any of these keys, it is paramount that you use these principles for the good of all. There is a hidden intelligence from which we all operate and that intelligence knows when and for what we are asking. If you are asking for harm to come to someone else, harm *may* come to you. Also, you do not need to "take" what belongs to another, for there is enough for all of us. All we need to do is ask. Ask yourself. Give yourself permission to receive that which you ask for. Our innate goodness inside wants for each one of us to be happy, prosperous and in balance. These things and many more, such as Love and Harmony, are all thoughts we can hold in our mind on a daily basis. It is with these thoughts that we can truly change the world in which we live. When we hold such thoughts our personal life begins to change, and then we notice the world around us beginning to change. It is in that change we truly receive the gifts of the Universe.

Here is your Key to unlocking the mystery of attracting your desires.

Remember what Raymond Holliwell said:

"Desire connects you to the thing desired and expectation draws it into your life."

Start by listing out your desires. Those things you have most wanted in your life. Please keep in mind to use this key or universal law to harm another will only bring negative energy back to you. So please use this only to draw good to you and not to take away from another.

If you are not sure what to start with then just practice something simple like finding the perfect parking place, as you read about. The way this works best is when it is genuine or you really have to be "there" or you truly want to go. Non-the-less, it is fun to experiment with just to see how powerful you really are in creating what you want.

Once you have your desire in mind, i.e. "I am going shopping today at the South Center Mall and I need to be on the Sears end" then have great expectation that the perfect parking place will manifest. You may not believe this yet but enter into it with confidence and watch what happens. If it is not happening then I would suggest that you are harboring some doubt about whether this can happen.

When you are able to manifest your desired good then it means you have and are aligned with your higher self. Be sure to keep a journal of the experiences so you can know when you were aligned with your higher self and when you were not. It is in the knowing of "when" you are aligned that you can recognize and move into manifesting your desired good on a daily basis.

A PERSON'S TRUE CHARACTER IS REVEALED BY WHAT HE DOES WHEN NO ONE IS WATCHING.

ANONYMOUS

Chapter Three

The Keys to Giving & Receiving

> Although it is true that everything you will ever want is already here, it is up to you to get into harmony with it. Clearly, you will never get into harmony with prosperity, if you insist on holding images of lack and limitation in the storehouse of your marvelous mind. Since you are always magnetized toward something, it follows it can never be anyone else's fault, when something comes into your life you supposedly do not want. Understand you have ordered it and it is being delivered to you right on schedule!
> From: <u>You Were Born Rich</u> by Bob Proctor

Mr. Proctor is saying all that you currently receive in your life is there because you ordered it and you created it. All you have read up until now has said the same thing. You held a thought in your mind telling the Universe "This is what I want." The Universe responded and you attracted it to you. If it is something you did not want then you tend to say, "I didn't want this in my life." In essence, what you have said to the universe is "No, thank you, I do not want to receive this now," even after you have asked for it. It is because of the *lack of gratitude* that we begin to realize fewer and fewer of our desires. What we need to do is learn to be *grateful for all* that we receive, even in the face of tremendous challenges. When we understand there is a bigger picture than we can see and know there is good in all situations, we can then receive all that we ask for with grace.

What is the first step for getting into harmony with prosperity and abundance so we can receive the gifts the universe has waiting for us?

There are many areas in which to start, such as looking at how we treat others or how we see ourselves in life. I think the most important area we must bring into harmony is our health. If we are not receiving into our bodies that which we need to stay healthy, then how can we receive the other gifts that Divine Intelligence has waiting for us? When your body is not healthy, it is not in divine order.

> William Warch says in his book, <u>How to Use Your Twelve Gifts from God</u>: "Your body temple is a human mechanism, which contains Spirit as your soul. As a mechanism, it is completely obedient to your consciousness. Like a computer, if it receives improper programming, it will go out of order or break down."

What kind of programming have you received? Is it the kind of programming that brings into your life the things *you say* you do not want? How could you not want them or receive them? If we are holding thoughts of lack, as Bob Proctor mentioned in the above statement, how can we expect to receive anything different? The thoughts you have been putting out to the universe, to the Divine Intelligence, to God, as I choose to call this Power, are no different than that of a radio operator. The radio operator inputs whatever he or she wants to talk about into a system of electronics and sends out a vibration or frequency into the air, which is then picked up at another location by way of receiver. Your thoughts and desires are sent out much in the same manner and received by the Spiritual Intelligence. That intelligence then sends back to you a physical manifestation of what you were thinking. It was given to you whether you said you wanted it or not. Because you held that image in the forefront of your mind, the mind's eye, the universe responded to your request. The captain of your ship, your unconscious mind, went to work to bring to you what you have asked for.

Let's take a look at how well you receive. The following story illustrates an opportunity for each one of us to notice what thoughts and feelings surface around money and the receiving of money. Carefully observe any feelings and emotions you experience as you imagine you are the recipient of a large amount of money.

Imagine you are sitting at home having a relaxing evening when you hear a knock on the door. You get up to answer and find there is no one there. Upon further investigation you notice a large chest or footlocker outside your door with a note attached to it. On the note are your name and a statement that reads, "This is for you." You drag it inside because it is too heavy to carry. You sit down with the chest in front of you and open it. What you see inside is lots of money. More money than you have ever seen. There are thousands of dollars in neatly wrapped twenty-dollar bills. There is enough money to take care of you for the rest of your life. What is the first thought that goes through your mind? Are you elated? Are you thinking you can finally do all you have ever dreamt of? After a few minutes with this money, do you began to worry about someone else discovering it? You think; I'd better hide it or hire a guard so no one takes it from me. What if the guard is dishonest? Hire another guard, you can afford it. Before long you might begin to think this much money brings more problems because of all you need to do to keep it. What feelings and emotions are you experiencing now?

Please note that the money itself is innocent. It can neither bring you problems nor fix the ones you have. Every problem you think the money will bring is only a belief you have about money. This would be a good time to write down what you observed. The beliefs you carry inside about money are related to and determine how well you receive all the gifts in your world.

I hope you have an idea of how you've received the things you did not want in this life as well as the things you did. In order for you to have received what you may or may not have wanted, you first *gave* in some way, whether you knew it or not. How we truly receive, is first done by giving. What is meant by giving?

You may have heard this verse before; "Give and it shall be given unto you good measure, pressed down, shaken together and running over." (From Luke 6:38) When you give, you open up an area of your life that may have been blocked by too many things; therefore, you had no room to receive any other good.

When I lived in Seattle, Washington for 3 years, I did not have many friends and I did not have an abundance of extra-curricular activities to attend. Now, I am not an unfriendly person. I could not figure out why I wasn't making as many friends as I had before I moved to Seattle. I thought like many of us would think at first, "Oh, it has to be the kind of people that live here. Everybody is too busy for a new friend." In reality, it was the kind of energy or thought I was giving to the world around me. What I received back was the lack of new friends.

I also did not give my time anywhere, as a volunteer. I have since found that when you *give* your time to any project that betters humanity, you receive rewards beyond your imagination.

It wasn't until I moved to Portland, Oregon and found a spiritual home that I really immersed myself in giving my time in everything I could possibly volunteer in. I became available at every turn to really assist my spiritual home. I helped out in the bookstore, I wrapped pipes so they wouldn't freeze, and I have been on what we call the hospitality team since I arrived. I made a decision to give for the first time in my life without wondering what I am going to get in return. I share this with you since it is in the volunteering, the giving of my time, that the universe has given to me so many wonderful friendships. I wouldn't trade it for anything.

Giving of your time offers a healing in areas of your life that may need to take place. Although it can be difficult to give when you are in need of comfort, give, give to others, and give your time and your talent. In the giving of yourself in your time of need and/or grief it will feel uncomfortable maybe even unsettling because you feel like you have nothing to give. Give anyway. In the giving,

it is easier to stay out of Gods way so she can do the work in your life that needs to be done.
Giving offers fulfillment at a time when all we feel is a sense of emptiness.

When we give we must give without worrying about what we are going to get. Getting is not a Spiritual law. Giving is. Once again, in order to receive, we must give. Raymond Holliwell states in his book, <u>Working with the Law</u>, *"Giving, which is the <u>first</u> or fundamental law of Life, is the <u>first</u> law of all creation."* Read that again. If it is true that giving is the first law of Life, then why is it we tend to hold onto things that no longer serve us? Do you really need to keep that coat you've only worn once in the last year or two? Is it so important to you that you cannot *give* or share it with someone else? What about the old habits and programming you have been holding onto?

Does that thought of Harry ripping you off ten years ago really serve you any longer? What about the anger you hold inside for the person that broke your heart four and a half years ago? It has been said, "holding onto anger is like taking poison yourself and expecting the other person to die." Could you imagine what is happening to your body by harboring ill will toward others? How would you act knowing what you put out to the Universe, you receive ten-fold? What areas of your life or your body are not responding to life, because you are holding onto possessions, emotions or habits that no longer serve you?

Please keep in mind that I am not saying you will be struck down if you do not give up your old clothes or possessions. I am merely stating that by not giving up those things that no longer serve you,

you will not make room for the new in your life. If you are to make room for all your desires, it is imperative to release those things that block the flow of good yet to come. Think about this. I'm fairly certain that most of us have been caught in a traffic jam. The flow of traffic is blocked because somewhere there is too much traffic to allow a smooth flow of vehicles to move freely. At one time or another we have all felt our lives have been in a traffic jam. Only when we move the things that are blocking the flow of good, can we receive that good.

    You may be saying, "Ok, I can give up some of my old items to make room for the new, but what do I do with the old habits, conditioning or anger? I certainly don't want to give that to anyone else." Very true, you certainly don't. The best suggestion I can give you is to release it to the Universe. Give it to the Universe and as you do say these words: I give this _____?_____ over to the Universe and send it out where it can be used for growth wherever it is needed. Keep in mind that the emotion you are releasing is energy. <u>E</u>nergy in <u>M</u>otion = E-motion. Please note that you may need to do this several times in order to be complete. I might recommend having a counselor you can work with if this seems too emotional. Now that you have released that energy you have opened a place in you that now has room to receive the new you wish for in your life. Our lives are like sponges. When a sponge is full, it is full. You could not put more water in it even if you submersed it. Once you squeeze the water out of the sponge, you have room for more water.

As it is with our lives, we can only absorb so much before we need to release and let go in order to have the space for more of what we desire.

What about money? Have you ever given a portion of your money to a good cause or a charity? How is it by giving money that we receive more abundance? As it was mentioned above it is in the giving, truly giving, that we receive. I might add that when you give, you must give from the heart, not the wallet. You will not always receive exactly that which you put out. Let me explain. Let's say, as an example, you decide to give $50.00 to a local charity. Once you give that $50.00 you release it and let it go with no attachment. A few days later you receive a piece of art that you have been admiring for sometime that has a value of $80.00. Do you see how that worked? You will not necessarily receive money as a return. The universe will respond in equal or greater value. Once again, you must detach yourself from the outcome. We will talk about detachment in the next chapter.

Please keep in mind that if you plan on giving your time, your talent or your treasure you must find an outlet where you can give without end for if you give in a patchy manner then you will receive in a patchy or sporadic manner. It will not be consistent because neither you nor I have been consistent. What we are telling that Spiritual Mind is, "I'll give to you here but I won't give to you there," or "I'll give later but I can't give now." Once again, the Universe responds in like kind. When you give a portion of what you have you are telling the universe that you have plenty. As you begin giving you will create a vacuum in your life-meaning that you open up a hole, a gap that is just waiting to be filled. The universe will fill that gap with your desires. (Please note: I am not suggesting giving money if it means not paying your rent or other bills. Please use your discretion as you begin to give money.)

All you need to do is: 1) make your desires known, 2) expect them to manifest, 3) detach from them. 4) *Give* thanks in advance. In the detachment and gratitude you are expressing to the Universe your trust in that Intelligence to manifest your desires.

I "give" you the Key
to Giving and Receiving.

In order to unlock the mystery of giving and receiving you must look at what you are giving out in the world. If what you are receiving is not what you want then look at what you are giving.

Are you giving out criticisms to others or are you showing them kindness?
The world is our mirror. What we see in others we see in ourselves. If you are criticizing others then that is what you see in yourself. If you give out kindness then that is what you will get in return.

Are you holding onto emotions that no longer serve you, therefore giving out hurt or maybe anger?

Do you need more time in your life? Have you ever given or volunteered your time anywhere? It is amazing how this works. I challenge you to give your time, 10% of your work hours, to some charitable organization for 60 days and watch how much more time you come up with.

Do you need more money in your life? Have you ever considered tithing to the place you get your spiritual nourishment? Tithing means 10%. The key here is not to hold the physical place in mind but to hold and know in your mind that what you give circulates to do greater work in and around our world.

What are your talents? Do you donate your talents to assist others? Are you a musician? You may want to consider giving your time and talent at a hospital or retirement center. Are you a carpenter? You may want to consider giving your time assisting others to remodel someone's home when they are not capable.

      Remember, what you give must be from your heart and not given just for getting. This tends to work in reverse. When you are ready to give from your heart you will know where and how much time, money and talent to give.

Trust your intuition.

"OUR BACKGROUND AND CIRCUMSTANCES MAY HAVE INFLUENCED WHO WE ARE, BUT WE ARE RESPONSIBLE FOR WHO WE BECOME."

ANONYMOUS

Chapter Four

The Keys to Detachment

What is exactly meant by detachment? The word actually means the act of detaching or separating, the state of being detached of the abstraction from worldly objects. We will look mostly at the later part of this meaning. Please keep in mind we will focus upon detachment from more than worldly objects. It is imperative to remember there are states of emotions that we all need to detach from as well if we are to move forward in our lives and in this world in the manner in which we desire.

Before you make your desires and intentions known you need to look at what can be renounced in your emotional life. Renunciation is another form of detachment. It is your ability to forgive and release others as well as release the negative beliefs, thoughts and feelings from your consciousness. Renunciation, as well as giving, creates a vacuum in your life and prepares an opening for more of the good that is waiting to come to you. The following story is a perfect example of renunciation.

Like many kids growing up in the last fifty years I, too, had parents that divorced. After a few years of being divorced my mother met a man who eventually became my stepfather. He was a hard worker and always kept food on the table and paid the bills. As a result of his own upbringing, he was an angry man. Beneath that anger was a lot of pain and that anger caused a lot of pain and hurt in our lives. When I asked my mother why he was so angry she commented that he lived in too much darkness and that was all he knew. Unfortunately he never moved passed the darkness in his life. Anger, in conjunction with his heavy smoking, played a role in his health continually deteriorating.

A couple of years ago my stepfather made his transition from this world. As a war veteran, the Veterans Administration Office made his funeral arrangements. The VA's office called my mother and gave her the choice of a below ground or above ground burial. My mother's response was one of compassion at its highest level. She told the VA's office she wanted him above ground, facing the rising sun because he had had enough darkness in his life. She wanted him to experience the Light in his death.

It was in that act of compassion that my mother was able to renounce the pain associated with that relationship, and detach from it. In her detachment she experienced freedom from the past.

If you are to experience freedom from your past pain and hurt and have what you want in your world, the next thing to do is to set an intention to manifest what you want, whether it is material or healing or freedom from the past. (Making a decision is another form of setting an intention). All sorts of reading material on intention can be found as well as what has been mentioned in an earlier chapter. Once you know what you want, have set your goals and made your intentions known to the Universe, you must release it and let it go. That doesn't mean you quit working toward that which you desire, you simply let it go and detach yourself from the outcome.

Reverend Mary Manin Morrissey says, "Sometimes when you get caught up in the energy of *'its got to happen now,'* you end up pushing away the very thing you desire." That is the result of attachment.

We have been taught that once we decide what we want, we should go for it with all our might. This kind of thinking has led to all kinds of competition and animosity toward others. We have been taught since we were kids that all the things we want in our life come from one source *or* another. From those teachings we believe that our employer is the source of our paychecks or the car lot is the source of the cars we drive. We have been cultured to believe that the farmer is the source of our food or the stores are the source of the material items we buy. This is not so. We are all *channels* through which the One Source works. We all have a higher source known as Divine Guidance, God, or Spiritual Intelligence; no matter what you choose to call it, we are, if we open to it, a channel for that Source. It is in recognizing the connection with this Source that we bring to each other our unique gifts and talents.

Once you move into knowing unquestionably all the things that are created in our lives come from the One Source, you can detach from the outcome of how you think things should be and move into a fuller expression of life. There is a Higher Source in this universe that assists you in moving into the true expression of who you are.

As we remain attached in our lives, that attachment colors how we look at the outcome.

We have been taught that once we determine what it is we want, we tend to hold onto the idea of how it needs to develop. Because we hold onto and value what we *think* is ours in life, we become prisoners of those items and/or emotions. Sometimes we become obsessed with something or someone to the point that is unhealthy. The meaning of obsession is: A preoccupation with a fixed idea or *unwanted* feeling of emotion accompanied by symptoms of anxiety of irrational repetitive actions against our will. When you think about it, is it worth it to hold onto things or emotions that block the flow of not only our energy, but also the energy of the universe? When energy is blocked by that which we hold onto, we are not open to receive the good the Universe wants to give us.

The following are examples that show how holding onto negative energy that no longer serves us blocks our good. The first is a true story that began when I was five years of age.

I remember one sunny day walking out into our front yard and preparing to play on the grass. As I approached the area I chose to play in I noticed a bumblebee in the grass. Since I didn't see any movement I thought the bee was dead. I wanted to make sure so I stomped on him- barefooted. As you might imagine I was stung and through the eyes of a child, the swelling of my foot looked bigger than life itself. I was instantly angry at the bee, because my day of play was ruined. It wasn't until twelve years later that I realized the depth of emotion and anger I held toward that bee when a friend and I were walking down a path to a pasture (after school). I witnessed a yellow jacket fly under a piece of plywood that had been lying on top of some loose hay. In a split second, that unconscious memory surfaced and I was taking action against that bee from so many years ago. I ran and jumped on that piece of plywood to kill the yellow jacket that really had nothing to do with the bee sting from long ago. Without warning, what seemed to be a hundred yellow jackets began swarming in a fury. There was a nest under that piece of wood and I had disturbed their daily duties. Suddenly, yellow jackets were flying up my pant legs. I had never moved so fast to remove my boots so I could get my jeans off. When all of the commotion had settled I discovered nine stings on my legs.

    What is the moral of this story? This is an enormous metaphor for how you can get stung in life, years later, if you harbor any negative emotions such as anger or resentments towards those people or things that may have hurt you in the past.

    Another example is writing this chapter. I started out thinking I knew what the end product of this subject was to be. Since I was attached to the outcome, I found it difficult to get started. My creative juices were just not flowing. A recent challenge was the ending of my relationship-as I mentioned in the first chapter. I was having a real tough time letting go of what could have been a very playful life. I loved this woman like I never thought I could ever love. At first I began to wonder why I loved her. At that time in my life I believed the feelings I was having were that of love. I realized later in a conversation with a very good friend that what I was really experiencing was the feelings of being accepted. It was, as you have read, a very difficult time in my life and to me it felt like all of life was rejecting me and as she accepted me, I equated that acceptance with love. I became attached to what I thought it should look like. It was that attachment and my insecurities that played a part in the relationship ending. I say played a part because each person brings his or her own "stuff" to the table in any relationship. I also attached meaning to some very old ways of what I thought love meant. One of them being that if you love, you will always get hurt. It was that belief that set up a fear of surrendering to the love she wanted to give. In other words, I was attached to some old ways of thinking and feeling.

When I finally detached from the old way of thinking, I could *really feel* her love, which by that time was too late. Make a conscious effort to detach yourself from those things that keep you captive before it is too late in your life.

There is one area of our lives that tends to hold us more captive than any other. That is the area of *control*-whether it is us who is controlling or another person who is doing the controlling. There was a part in my relationship I know I controlled out of my fear. I also know there was a portion of the relationship where my partner was controlling because of her fears.

An example of controlling can be as minor as one person telling the other they are not doing "it" right or as major as saying something like, see what you did to me. Someone who is physically controlling another is a person that has a lot of fear built up inside. Fear around "losing" a part of himself or herself to something or someone else.

> When you first start a relationship, you are greatly attracted to your partner. They thrill and excite us. As you move further along in the relationship, things that excited us become the very things that threaten us. You try to control them, to shut down the area of attractiveness, because you want them to share it only with us and not anybody else. Of course, doing this does not work. When you shut down the attractiveness in any area, it begins to shut down in every area. Controlling our partner to make them feel safe also makes them dull. You create your own boredom. <u>If It Hurts, It Isn't Love,</u> Chuck Spezzano, Ph.D.

When you are detached from the outcome and are willing to give up control and allow your partner to be attractive you may feel threatened, and fear could possibly surface out of your own insecurities. To move past the fear, communicate that fear with your partner. Most fears you feel around partnerships are about the anxiety of them leaving. Just let them be who they are and fully enjoy them.

We also become attached to the material things. When we set a goal to have a certain item in life, we tend to stay so focused upon that item we push it away-as Rev. Morrissey said in her statement. We also become attached to the things we already have in our lives. Sometimes we are so afraid to let current items go because we "*think*" it is all we have, and we fear what *might* happen without it.

While you are in the attachment phase and connected more with the outcome, you are not in connection with your higher self or the Divine Source of all. Once you connect with the Source and detach yourself, you can readily move in the direction of your dreams. Once connected, and detached from the outcome, then I could readily put into words what the Spiritual Intelligence (God) wants all of us to know.

Anything you want can be acquired through detachment, because detachment is based on the unquestioning belief in the power of your true Self. Attachment on the other hand, is based on fear and insecurity; and insecurity is based on not knowing your true Self. The source of wealth, of abundance, or of anything in the physical world is the self. This statement comes from a very highly recommended book, <u>The Seven Spiritual Laws of Success,</u> by Dr. Deepak Chopra

When you start moving into and acknowledging there has been attachment in your life, you have taken the first step in detaching yourself from the outcome. The second step is to absolutely trust the Universe. If you have a hard time "trusting the universe," then trust your heart. When you are truly connected they *are* the same. When you move into trusting your heart, you are saying, "I trust myself, which is trusting in the Spirit of God."

If you don't believe me, then try it for yourself. Make a decision about something in your life or do something that you have felt in your heart for quite some time. Once you have made that decision from the heart, trusting that your heart *is* connected to the Higher Source, detach yourself and your ego from what you think the outcome should be and go about your day giving gratitude for that which is moving toward you.

"Without total trust, it is impossible to know the miracle of the higher self and manifest what you want in your life." From <u>Manifest Your Destiny</u> by Dr. Wayne Dyer.

Please keep these things in mind, especially if you have lived with a lack of trust for a long time. 1) All of us were taught to believe one way or another; therefore, we have different perceptions about what may seem like the same thing. 2) As with learning anything new, it may not be easy for you to trust wholeheartedly. Don't be too hard on yourself and least of all, don't judge yourself because you think you are not doing it right. Be open.

It takes time. You didn't just go for a nice long ride on the first bike you ever tried to ride. You had to learn to balance before you could ride on your own. Once you began to get your balance you felt good about it. You felt like you could ride anywhere.

The same principle applies with learning to trust in you. If you have not known how to trust and feel like you are on a bike for the very first time, out of balance, be assured, once you open to the trust, you will feel that sense of balance as you did on that first bike. It is in the balancing of all areas of your life that you will begin to have a sense of peace throughout your life.

Each day as you trust in yourself more and more, you will be able to detach from the outcome of everything you desire. There is a certain amount of freedom that comes with detachment. Start by freeing yourself today of at least one fixation you've carried around for a long time. Commit to detaching yourself from something today, be it emotional or the material items you've held onto that no longer serve you. Make your desires known and detach from them as well.

Make your intentions known to the Spiritual Intelligence by writing out your dreams and desires and stating, "this or something better." Once you tell God what you want, prepare to receive it. What do I mean by that? If you really want to reach your intended goal (desire) then you can't just "wait" for it. You must prepare the way. A farmer would not think of planting next year's crop without preparing the field. It is no different with us. You must prepare your field if you expect the Universe to respond to your desires. Plant your seeds and nurture them. Your seeds are your dreams and desires. You nurture them daily by stating in the present moment as if you have already received the item of your desire.

If you do not prepare to receive that which you have stated, and detach yourself from it, you are telling the universe you are really not ready to accept all you have asked for. How many of you have seen someone receive just what he or she wanted and said, "Are they ever lucky!" The meaning of luck is "when opportunity meets the prepared mind." Benjamin Franklin. Do you want to feel luckier in your life?

Then state what you want, prepare the way, and you will surely have what you ask for.

Now that you have detached yourself from the outcome and placed the trust where it belongs, in your heart instead of your head, give gratitude for all that is preparing to come to you before it gets here. When you show gratitude before you receive any of the things you have asked for, you are telling the universe that you trust in it and it will bring to you what you have asked for, or something better. State what you want, detach from it, trust in the Higher Intelligence and give gratitude before it arrives.

Here is your Key to Detachment

Ask your self what you are holding onto that you no longer need.

no — Do you have a closet full of clothes that you haven't worn in years? By cleaning out all your closets you make space for new things to enter into your life.

no — Are you holding onto anger or resentment from an old relationship or toward a parent or sibling? My guess is that if you are or have been harboring these feelings and emotions your physical health could be out of harmony with your desired picture of you as a healthy person.

By releasing these thoughts through the forgiveness process your health will begin to return. Additionally, when you release these feelings you will notice the people around you responding to you in a different manner.

yes — How is the overall appearance of you home? Is it cluttered or do you have "stuff" all about your house that could be released? How about your garage? What does it look like? How about your yard? Is it an invitation or a sign that states stay away?

no — How about your kitchen? Do you have science projects growing in your refrigerator?

All of these things block new good from coming into your life. You will find that when you clean out all areas in your life, external as well as internal, you will notice a shift in your life towards a more positive living experience.

CHILDREN MAY CLOSE THEIR EARS TO
ADVICE, BUT OPEN THEIR EYES TO EXAMPLE.

ANONYMOUS

Chapter Five

The Keys to Gratitude

"Up until now!" That is a small but powerful statement. What does it mean?

Before I answer that, let's take a look at what is in your life. Do you have a place to sleep? Do you have a place to go to work even if it is not your ideal job? What about clean water to drink or a place to take a shower? Have you given gratitude for all that you have in your life regardless of what it looks like? Are you living in a small rented place and keep wishing you had a bigger or better place to live? Do you give gratitude for that small place that keeps you safe? A lack of gratitude can result in a lack of the life you desire to live. You can start right now, right this very moment, and say, "Up until now I have not said thank you for all that you do. I now give gratitude for the life you have given me." (If it feels strange to think about saying thank you to you don't know what, once again, imagine a picture of the whole universe in your mind and say, "Thank you.")

Please keep in mind that sincerity is the intention that carries gratitude to creating a better life; and communicating gratitude to the universe is what brings that better life to us. In addition to communicating gratitude to the Infinite Mind, take a look at how you "see" your life and the role you are playing. Are you grateful for all the lessons you have learned to get you to where you are? Look for all the good in every moment even if you can't see it right away. As with building the trust to ride a bicycle, this will require some practice. Take it one step or one situation at a time.

I can assure you if you open to finding the good, any good, you will see it, and just like magic, your world begins to look different.

At the same time I was terminated from my job the thoughts of this book started entering my mind. That night before my dismissal, two of my friends told me about a position with a company that paid considerably more money and would offer some travel. I told them I really was not interested since I was working for a company that I enjoyed. However, they saw greater things for me and for that reason I told them I would call. The next day I was canned. I was certainly stunned; since I had no idea this was about to happen. Amazingly, I gave great gratitude for this divine opportunity as I was walking out the door.

I was never worried since I had come to learn and know in my life, that God has great things planned for us if we will just trust Her. I met with the owner of the business the following Wednesday and after a great interview I was offered the position, in writing. I accepted the position since I believed and trusted that God has a greater plan for all of us if we will just open to the greater good.

Now I know some of you might be saying that I was just lucky. Remember that luck is when preparation and opportunity come together. Even though I was not actively seeking, I remember a few statements I made that the Universe heard and honored. Probably the most important one is, "I want to attend ministry school." However, that old job did not provide enough income to make that happen.

Divine Intelligence heard and answered. By preparing the way with that statement and the completion of the application process into the ministry school, the opportunity showed itself at the perfect time. I am extremely grateful for this position because of the wonderful fit for both the company and myself. I do not believe any of us could have orchestrated this change without being connected to the Source. This takes us back to the opening statement, which is what I said, "Up until now God, I have not known how to make this work so I turn it over to you." I gave gratitude and moved forward. I showed my appreciation to that Intelligence before I stepped one foot inside the new office. Everyday I do the work it takes to operate within the Laws of the Universe, the laws that govern our lives. That is how the new position showed up so quickly.

You've all heard the expression, "an attitude of gratitude." Do you have one? How would you know? Let's take a look at some of the ways that both keep you out of gratitude and in gratitude.

In order to understand gratitude and the lack of it, we need to understand the split personality, so to speak, between the ego and the spirit that dwells within each of us. Imagine this for a moment. You are enjoying a nice evening in your back yard. You have two kids. They were born twins. You are watching them play and all of a sudden you notice a difference between them. At first it seems trivial. You notice one of the children "taking" toys from the other child, all the while stating in a firm voice that what he is taking "belongs" to him. The basic belief demonstrated here is that there will not be enough and the child wants to take and hang onto as much as possible. The other child is gladly sharing without resisting, demonstrating the knowledge that there will be enough to go around, that there *will* be more, and could possibly be better.

This is what it is like between the ego and the spirit. The ego wants to hang on while the spirit that dwells within *all* of us is grateful for what it has and gives graciously and receives gratefully. When we act in line with our true spiritual nature, life seems to come and go without worry. When acting from ego, satisfaction is never attainable.

I share this with you because "up until now" I have lived that kind of life. When I tell you that it is a path without end, I mean that when you are not satisfied and demonstrating a lack of gratitude for what you have or where you are, regardless of what it looks like, your world *will* get smaller. If any of you grew up in what seemed to you at the time to be a world of lack, that is how you might react to the world around you due to your early programming. Even if you grew up in a secure home you may still experience feelings of lack in your life. It may be lack of emotional security and/or Love.

I have also experienced this in my own life. When my father left, my mother had six kids to rear. She was laid off from her nursing job and had a difficult time finding another one. We had to live on welfare until she met the man who became my stepfather. There were a lot of times when we had to share only what was available. It seemed like there was never enough to go around. Without knowing it, we were being programmed with a "lack consciousness." I don't blame my mother, she did the best she could with the knowledge she had.

When my stepfather entered our lives he brought his three kids. It seemed like things became even scarcer, since there were eleven people in the same house, even though we were no longer on welfare.

When we are programmed with these kinds of thoughts for years, it often shows up in our current life. Have you ever asked the question, "What does it take for me to get the things I want in my life?" The answer is gratitude for all that you have had in your life "up until now." The splendor of giving gratitude is like waking and walking into a new day, everyday. Give gratitude for all you have, including the hardships in your life. Without them you would not be who you are today. Who you are today has been shaped by whom you have been. "If you want to know who you are, it is important to know who you've been." Dax, from Star Trek, Deep Space Nine. When you know who you've been, then you can decide in which direction you would like to take your life.

What stops us from experiencing more gratitude in our lives? It is how we currently see life. Are you looking at your life and the life of those around you through judgmental eyes? Do you look for the faults in others instead of finding what's right with them? Do you complain about your life instead of giving gratitude for it? Have you decided that everything in your life is already established and arranged? In other words, do you take everything for granted? If so, these are some of the reasons your life is not working the way you want it to. There are many reasons your life is not proceeding, as you would like it to. Let's look at some key areas.

It has been said many times that we are mirrors for each other. In other words, what you see in others, you are really seeing or recognizing as part of yourself.

When you see someone as kind, loving and caring then that is a "part of you" you recognize. When you are judging or being critical of others as well, you are also noticing a part of you, which you don't like and may be choosing not to express.

Think about a time when you were judging someone. Look at what you were judging them for. Now, look deeply into yourself and you may find something that you actually disliked about yourself. You may not like it or even want to believe it, but if you stay with it you will find a piece of yourself you really want to enhance or maybe let go of. Give gratitude to the Divine Intelligence for revealing to you that which has held you from growing into your higher self.

Those people that come into our lives show up to reveal the next step in our growth. They did not show up for us to judge them. When we meet someone we should be asking the question, what could this person show or teach me about myself? It is synchronous we meet the people we meet just when our life seems to need that person. We don't know why they fascinate us or why we may not like them, but our spirit knows. I personally believe we make agreements with those who come into our lives at a spiritual level before we incarnated on this earth plain. If that statement offends some of you, please know that once again I do not challenge your personal beliefs. However, I believe this is one reason why we are captivated by some people and not others. Our souls "know" each other. Neale Donald Walsh has a children's book entitled: <u>The Little Soul & The Sun.</u> It is a great synopsis of the possibility of how we meet before we meet. I highly recommend this read.

Each one of us has a choice to either find fault or find what is right in our lives and the lives of those around us. When you look for the faults in others, you are really seeking out what is missing in your own life, and focusing on what is not acceptable about your life. This is the ego's way of denying the growth opportunity in us by saying, I am better than that person and to prove it I will tell them what is wrong with them. This can show up in a number of ways, but the most destructive manner is anger. As long as we focus on what is wrong and what is missing in the lives of others, we will continue to "see" what is wrong and what is missing in our lives and that is exactly what we will manifest. "Energy flows where attention goes." Huna or Hawaiian philosophy.

Do you want to participate in the co-creation of your life? Start by showing gratitude for what you have. If you have a notion or feeling to compliment someone then do it. Tell them what you find fascinating about them. One of the best ways to do this is to let the other person talk about him or herself and to encourage that person, even if you don't know them.

How much of your life has been given away by taking the people and things in your life for granted? Throughout our lives we have all taken things and people for granted. This is the ego's way of disconnecting from the interest we have for someone or something because it thinks it is already settled. Instead of enjoying the moment, the ego creatively finds ways to avoid "that" which truly feeds and fulfills our very soul. This is called *"creative avoidance."*

    The Ego is constantly looking for "more" so we fall into this trap that the more we have the better off we will be. In reality we begin to feel emptiness no matter how much "more" we have acquired. By continuing to live in that "take it for granted" stage of our lives, we are truly missing or will miss that unexpected gift from the Universe which marks the beginning of the new life you have been asking for, for years.

    Complaining is another barrier that keeps us from living our lives to the fullest potential. This is probably one of the ego's biggest weapons against gratitude. When we or those around us constantly complain, we are actually telling the Universe that we want more-like some spoiled little child who never has enough. You could feed the ego everything it ever wants in one day and by tomorrow it won't be enough.

    Living from and for the ego is like working for a boss who is never satisfied, always telling you he needs you to do more, get more, but never telling you to *be more*. This is the very thing the ego fears. To *be more* is to have more. The lists of demands never end. Just like the un-grateful boss, the ego fears it will be left behind. So the ego, in an attempt to fill your world with all it thinks it wants, is really feeling shortchanged. This is where complaining begins.

Complaining is an expression of the absence of love in your inner world. We get upset at the universe or God for not meeting our ego's demands. When you feel love, there is no room for being upset with God." From <u>Manifest Your Destiny</u> by Dr. Wayne Dyer.

"By becoming more satisfied, more grateful and more joyful, you will experience lightness in your life." Dr. Wayne Dyer. There is no room or reason for being upset with those we have invited into our lives.

Do you want your life to be different? If so, start today by expressing your gratitude for the things you currently have in your life, regardless of what it looks like. If you have a difficult time deciding what to be grateful for then just walk outside and watch children play or feel the grass under your feet. Make the time to watch a sunrise or sunset today and be grateful for the eyes you have been given to see a sight that could not be created by anyone else but God. Maybe you like quiet time but don't seem to get much. Take a few moments for yourself and show your gratitude for the few moments you have. Don't be surprised when you start noticing that you are receiving more quiet time after the gratitude you have shown. At your next meal, no matter what it is, show some gratitude for the food before you consume it. Have you thanked your creator for your life today, even if it is not what you expected? Have you ever thought that maybe there is a better plan for you if you just follow your heart?

Whatever you do, before you do it, STOP, and give a moment of gratitude. This is something you can do silently or aloud. However you choose to express gratitude, express it.

You are not here by mistake. All the things in your life are not some random convergence of molecules that happened to stop on your doorstep. You are here for a greater purpose. It is up to you to discover, to uncover what that purpose is. The best way to determine and reveal to you what your purpose is and where you are going in this life is to begin now by having an attitude of gratitude for *everything* in your life. In showing gratitude, your life *will* be propelled forward.

> Every single experience of life is an opportunity to experience an attitude of gratitude or its opposite, a feeling of ennui (boredom). It is always a choice. <u>Manifest Your Destiny</u> by Wayne Dyer.

When you make the choice to express gratitude for all in your life, then something else begins to happen, something as if by magic or miracle. You begin to sense and even see more Love in your world. That is what our inner knowing strives to return to as we move into and through our world. And as you begin to live within the Laws of Love then there is nothing that shall be impossible to you.

Here is your Key
To Gratitude

You can acquire the key to gratitude in any moment by making a decision to be still and think about all you have to be grateful for. Please keep in mind that gratitude is about the feeling not about the things.

If you are reading this then I will assume you are alive. Is being alive not something to be grateful for? If you are alive then that means that you are breathing. If you are breathing then that in and of itself is one of the greatest gifts to be thankful for. Without the ability to breathe we would not have life or the opportunity to Love and be Loved or make our dreams come true.

Let's start with the most basic questions.

How do you *feel* when you think about the people and things in your life?

What lessons have you learned from every person that has come into your life, whether they are still here or not?
Is the lesson that helped you grow and know yourself at another level something to be grateful for?

Have you considered what that lesson was? If not, I would suggest going back in your mind and look at where your relationships were when they started and where they are now.

What change took place in you?
What gift did you receive from that person and/or situation?

What physical gifts have you been given? Are you grateful for those gifts or do you wish you were given something else? If it truly is something you have no desire for then give gratitude that it came into your life and then pass it on to someone you know who could use it and would be grateful to have received the new gift.

Be grateful, daily, that you have been given an opportunity to express who you are and the gifts you have brought into this world. Find your gifts and show them to the world.

Above all else, be grateful that you have the awesome opportunity to Love today, no matter what your life looks like you can still share the Love that is a part of your core being with those around you and do it in a moment.

You make the choice.
Make the choice to have a BIG Day and all you desire will be yours!

Be
In
Gratitude

Don't seek love or lover —
Seek passion and true love will follow.

Bob Woods

Chapter Six

The Keys to Love
(Subtitled: The Keys to Increase)

There is a journey that all of us have taken many times in our lives. This is not a journey with a destination, although there are two destinations where we have been so many times, we couldn't begin to count the number of trips. None of us has ever physically bought a ticket to either place, but we have all paid the price innumerable times in order to return to one or the other. You cannot pay for a one-way fare. Included in the price, is a return trip. There is no time schedule for this excursion. However, you can choose which location you would rather spend most of your time. This is a journey that has led us to the crossroads of our way of doing things or doing God's will. It is a journey of balance between your thinking nature and your feeling nature. It is a journey between the heart and the head-approximately 18 inches-but can be one of the most life shattering or life enhancing journeys any of us can embark upon.

As you begin this journey with me, please know that I am not an authority on Love nor do I pretend to have all the answers. I know what moving into and through Love feels like and I share my experience and perceptions about an ancient power that is everlasting. This power has been around since the beginning of time and will remain long after all of us have left this physical realm. This is not about romantic love, although romance plays a role in showing us all how to move into Love's presence so we can accept not only our own lives but the lives of *all* those around us. True increase takes place when we move into Love's presence. Moving into and being in the presence of Love, we begin to notice an increase of the things that truly matter in our lives.

There are two aspects in this chapter that bring increase into all areas of life. The first one is Love and the second is Praise. Look at those two words. Love. Praise. Is it possible they are one and the same? Would you be able to give someone true praise without knowing or feeling Love for that person? Do you know that in giving praise to all the things and people in your life you increase your own capacity for Love as well as all your desires? Let's take a look at Love first.

We've all heard the little quotes that "Love is patient, Love is kind" but for most of us we equate the Love in those statements with emotions. We have been conditioned to believe that Love is emotionally based. Through societal conditioning we have lost touch with the real meaning of Love. Have you ever heard or sensed that Love is not an emotion? In order to understand Love we need to understand emotion.

Remember from Chapter Three the explanation of emotion?

E-motion = Energy in motion. Albert Einstein said, "Energy can neither be created or destroyed, it merely changes form." What does that mean?

Everything on this earth is made up of energy molecules. Those molecules are always in motion. The chair you are sitting on is made up of those molecules just as you and I are.

If you take a piece of the chair and a piece of your skin and put both under the microscope you will see, at the highest microscopic level, that the molecules in both are the same. Molecules have mass with varying elements and density, therefore, varying frequencies. Beyond that, is pure energy. I am not a scientist and leave that part of the topic to those who are. There is more available on this subject. Dr. Deepak Chopra explains it very well in his books. I encourage you to check your local bookstore for the titles that interest you. The difference between you and the chair you are sitting on is that your energy vibrates at a much faster rate and higher frequency than that of the chair. Slower vibration equals denser, heavier mass. Your energy is not as dense as that of the chair. It is in that frequency of vibration, unlike that of the chair, that we experience consciousness and become aware of that consciousness.

When you feel sensations in your body such as anger, frustration or fear, it is energy in your body; it is a frequency of vibration. That energy must go somewhere. You can turn that energy into a higher vibration that moves you toward the true meaning of Love. Love is the highest frequency or vibration we can obtain as conscious beings. As mentioned in the opening there are two destinations, Love and living from your heart is one of them.

If Love is not an emotion, the label we have given it, then what is it? Love is the *knowing* you are One with all. Love is like many talented singers coming together and harmonizing in an indescribable concert. Love is living in harmony with the world around us.

Love is living in harmony with spiritual principles. When we get to a place of desiring good for all, not just ourselves, that is Love. When you look at someone and bless him or her and wish for them their highest good, truly from your heart, you are expressing Love.

Most of us have been taught that unless people are the way we want them to be we cannot love them. That is conditional Love. We have been taught that we need to get our emotional needs met in order for us to love. The paradox is when we do get our emotional needs fulfilled; we put conditions on how to continue the fulfillment process. When we move into Oneness with all people, things and emotions, we can then avoid conditional Love.

To feel that Oneness, the real Love that is the oneness, create a balance between your thinking nature and your feeling nature. Both the thinking and feeling natures represent two energy fields in our body.

One is the feminine and the other is the masculine. However, some people think they don't have both energies.

When a male feels anything emotionally, it is felt through the feminine side of who he is. If a female has to absolutely put aside her emotions and begin to *think* about what to do in times of adversity, then she is in touch with her masculine side. According to the symbology of the Bible the male characteristics are the thinking nature of each one of us where the female characteristics are our feeling nature. In order to know the oneness with all we must increase our awareness and know that Love is expressed in our consciousness, through our feeling nature. When we express our feelings consciously, being totally aware and purposeful, we create the balance in our lives that opens us to all we desire.

There is another aspect of Love that will draw all things to you if you so desire. Do you love having enough food to eat more than you hate not having enough? Do you love having money more than you hate not having it? Do you love having your friends more than you hate the people that irritate you? If you have any emotions around Loving *anything or anybody* in your life it is time to look once again to your beliefs about those emotions. It is in Loving and showing love toward all things in life that we draw Love into our lives.

> Love is a spiritual gift, an ability to direct the power of the Spiritual Intelligence, God, for earthly good. Emotions come and go, but Love is never changing. Still yourself toward Love, to the point of fulfillment, then direct generously, enabling peace to be restored on earth. From: How to Use Your Twelve Gifts From God by William Warch.

Before we move on to the second part of the Keys to Increase, I would like you to know that what has been shared with you on Love is only a fraction of what can be experienced. I would encourage you to look toward other sources on the subject. One of the best I have found is a book and audiocassette entitled A Return to Love by Marianne Williamson.

What would you do to increase the good in your life and bring about more happiness and pleasure? How about freedom from the stresses of everyday irritating circumstances or people in and around you? What do I mean by people in you? Those people you believe have harmed you, you carry negative thoughts as baggage in you. You probably have tried a number of ways to end the never-ending story that continues to play in your head. There are two ways to complete that which no longer serves you or those around you. One is praise and the other is forgiveness. In Chapter Seven we will discuss forgiveness, which is something that releases past pains and baggage we bring into the present.

Praise is enmeshed and is one with Love. Praise is something you can do in a moment. Praise can and will alleviate having to *go back* and either give or ask forgiveness.

I believe the best place to start is by praising yourself and your body. You might think this is crazy but it is crazier not to do it. When you give self-praise you actually open to all kinds of healing that may need to take place within your physical and emotional self. When you take the time to praise your body, you invite physical healing into all parts of your body that are awaiting healing. Since I praise and give gratitude for my body, I rarely visit any doctor. I give thanks for my body and praise it as a gift for me. As a result, I move around freely in excellent health.

When you consciously praise those things in your life you will find that praise is like a magnet.

Through this inherent Law, when man praises, he opens himself upward to the Divine Mind. She lifts her consciousness to a higher realm and becomes a greater channel to receive the good that is ever waiting to come to her. Praise opens a little door in the mind that enables each one of us to draw closer to the Infinite Intelligence, God, and be attuned to the Divine forces that govern our lives. <u>Working With The Law</u> by Raymond Holliwell.

When you praise you are stimulating your mind and that stimulation quickens prayer, intentions, and transforms all the good into visible substances.

Jesus did not have much when he had to feed more than five thousand hungry people on a five loaves of bread and a two of fish. How did he do it? He praised what was there and along with his vision, desire and faith, he fed all of them. *Praise is faith in action.* In other words when you give praise to all that you desire you are saying to the universe that you have an undying faith that it will be delivered. Praise is complementary to faith. When Jesus said, "These things you will do and greater still," he did not mean everybody except you. He meant that you too have access to the power of faith that he was so in touch with. The Keys to Faith will be discussed in Chapter Eight.

If you don't have much to begin with, that is the perfect place to start. The universe does not recognize quantity. Praise what you have now, even if it *doesn't* seem like much. Praise it everyday. Praise all that you receive daily regardless of what it looks like to you. Praise what you also desire, as you give thanks in faith for all you are receiving. Show up in life today fully giving praise for all that is around you and in your life. In giving praise you are showing the Universe that you are worthy of receiving the gifts from the Divine and that you appreciate those gifts, no matter what they look like.

"Do we really put Love first in our lives? What do we put before God? Sometimes our anger is more important than God, or our resentment. Sometimes our judgment or being right is more important than God. And when it's more important than God, it means it's more important than being available to God, to Love in this moment. How do you put love first? By asking the question: What would Love do here? Then follow the guidance you receive."
Rev. Mary Manin Morrissey

Millions of people suffer with addictions. They are addicted to something. More often than not, that something/addiction is more important than Love or God. Yet, they cling to it and may even hate it and themselves. This has been called "spiritually bankrupt, or as I like to call it, "spiritually homeless." Love is absent. Praise, thanks and forgiveness can help restore the balance in your life's journey and restore the flow of Love energy in your life.

If you are having a difficult time giving praise and showing faith consider the possibility that some forgiveness work may need to be done. If you don't think there is any forgiveness work for you to do, then ask yourself, "Are you breathing?" We all have forgiveness work that needs to be done before we can move into the next phase of our life. Forgiveness is a very freeing experience. It is the focus of the next chapter.

I lead you into the next chapter with another poem I was honored to be the vehicle for. This poem sums up the gift we all have available to us for the asking.

Pass It Around

*There is a power in this universe
that reaches from
the heavens to the ground;
This power is greater than you or I
this power is Love,
so pass it around.*

*The power of Love is within us all,
it is the one true power
that can save us when we fall.
If we open our hearts and give more
than we receive,
the gift of Love will be ours
for all eternity.*

*It is true we reap what we sow,
so if Love is what you need
then take Love by the heart
and plant the seed.*

*If Love is what you want and desire
to keep it around,
then take this precious gift and
Pass it around.*

6-23-95

Here is your Key to Love.

The first question I would ask any one including myself around any situation is where do you spend more of your time, in your head or your heart?

There is no circumstance or situation that is bigger than Love or the Divine. If your current experiences are what some would call negative then make a decision to introduce Love into that situation and it will surely be transformed.

Are you in a romantic Love relationship and it seems like the romance has left? Is your partner less than what you would like to experience in your relationship? Since none of us can control what another thinks or feels then all we can do is to send that person Love. Hold that person in the Highest Order of Love and you will notice a shift, possibly in them, but definitely in yourself. (As a side note if you don't know what holding someone in Love looks like then imagine those people surrounded in pure white light for it is the light that transforms the dark). The shift will be in how you respond to them and what you do with that response. We all have a choice. We can either "react," which means to act in opposition to a force for a second time or to return the same force or we can "respond," which means answer of reply taking responsibility for our own actions and not the actions of others.

How is your work situation? Is your relationship with your boss or co-workers less then you would like? If so, I would suggest that before you enter work each day for a period of at least one week stop and offer each person a silent blessing of peace and wellness, joy and happiness, Love and prosperity. Do this without expectation and go about your day as if everything was all right and I promise you will notice things starting to look and be different.

How are you with your own family? If you really want to pass the test of learning what Love looks like at the highest order then your family is one of the best places to begin. It has been said that if you can Love your biological family then the rest of the world would be easy. Each person in our lives is a mirror for who we are and how we grow. The first mirrors given to us are from our own family. This shows us how to be in the world if we are open to "looking" at others as our mirrors.

You cannot introduce Love into any situation from you thinking nature. It must come from your heart or your feeling nature. The paradox is that you must begin "thinking" about what Love is and how you would like Love to show up in your life and how to send it forth from your heart. Look beyond what you see with your physical eyes and you will begin to see "real" Love. This is the true meaning of increase in all of our lives.

Once the game is over the king and the pawn go back in the same box.

Italian Proverb

Chapter Seven

The Keys to Forgiveness

By now, as an adult you are aware that to enter into your home, your car or even your work you must have a key. Whether it is a physical key or an electronic key, you must have the key to enter into the place you desire to be. In life it is the same. You must have a key to enter into the life for which you hunger. There is not one key. There are several keys each of us must obtain before we can enter into the many rooms that hold the answers we seek. The laws you have read up to this point are all keys to an awakened world. With each law you have become aware of you have placed another key on your key ring of life. However, I believe there is a master key that will open more doors for us than any other key. That is the master key of forgiveness. Forgiveness offers us ease of entry when it is time to open the subsequent doors of our growth.

When most of us think about forgiveness we tend to believe that we are forgiving someone for the hurt they have caused us is saying to them that what they did was OK. That misconception is the furthest thing from the truth. You do not forgive another person for *their* well being, you forgive them for *your* well being. It is in forgiveness that we find an indisputable amount of freedom, and isn't that what we all want, freedom from the pain and hurt? A certain amount of the pain and hurt we feel arises from the memories we continue to play over and over again. I have no doubt the events that have caused you tremendous pains are very real, as are my own. In the forgiveness and detachment, as discussed earlier, of the people and circumstances that caused me pain, I freed myself from that which kept me from my greater good. You too can free yourself to enter into the world of your greater good.

My own personal story probably does not differ too much from yours or yours too much from those around you. Just like you, I have spent time wrestling with the issues of relationships as well as parental issues. There is one relationship in particular that somewhat shaped me for the person I now am. That experience deepened my ability to be calm instead of "high-strung." The full details are less important than where the experience took me. For that reason, I tell you the following story. Please keep in mind as you read this story that I was in a tremendous amount of pain and hurt and acted out of fear, not Love.

It was about fifteen years ago that I met this lovely young French woman. We hit it off immediately. Our relationship was a whirlwind for about six months. We were high on each other and non-stoppable. After about six months this young lady "pulled" something on me that I thought was totally unforgivable. I was so devastated that I decided to ensure she hurt as much as I did. I was watching a late night talk show when one of the guests talked about a Halloween prank she played on her friends. I took it to heart and planned my strategy for payback.

In my years in the military I learned the art of rappelling down the side of mountains. I became efficient at making safety harnesses. I gathered up the materials I needed to play the role as "the hurt one." While this woman was at work I went into her garage and began making the harness I would need to keep me safe. I proceeded to make a noose and threw it over the rafters and then hooked the rope into the harness, which was under a large sweatshirt so she wouldn't see it. She arrived home and noticed something amiss; I could not help feeling like this was all wrong. I began to feel remorse and pity for her even though she had hurt me tremendously. As the ego thoughts surfaced again, I made that journey back to my head and knew she would call for help. While she was making that call I let myself down and left before she returned. My ego felt satisfied, but my heart knew that I was wrong. Even now in the retelling of this story, I feel anxiety around my lack of forgiveness. You can be assured that that anxiety is moving me into a space of asking for forgiveness, again, even as I write this, so I may unblock that part of my life, thus completing the healing in that part of me.

It is difficult to share this story because I am not proud of what I did. This is an event that came into my life so I could make a choice between forgiveness and revenge. Everything we do, we either do out of Love or fear. By choosing fear rather than Love, I had to go through other painful situations until I learned the art of forgiveness. I kept walking through the same door until the lesson was learned. When we move in the direction of vengeance, we not only hurt those that hurt us, we hurt ourselves even more. It is the fear based vengeful choices like my illustration that keep us from obtaining the key of forgiveness so we can enter into our desired world.

Another choice that prevents us from living as our true authentic selves is allowing the fear of abandonment to immobilize us. Often in relationships we tend to obsess with thoughts that the person(s) will leave us. In those thoughts we fail to fully express our true authentic selves.

The following story illustrates fear of abandonment and the forgiveness it took to move past that fear.

Jason, a friend of mine, was approaching seventeen years of age and from all societal standards his life was considered normal. He was a kid moving into adulthood and living with his mother, father and two brothers. One day Jason received news that his grandmother made her transition, from old age to the great beyond.

Shortly thereafter, his two brothers died-one brother died from an overdose of drugs and alcohol, and the other in a skydiving accident. Within a short period of time, his father passed away from cancer. If that wasn't enough, his mother, in her own deep pain and grief, took her life by asphyxiation in the garage. He knows now that it was too much for her and she wanted to end the pain. His life as he saw it, until years later, would never be "normal" again. In addition to the weight of these events, he was also left with the responsibility of adult decisions in the form of a house, two cars, an insurance policy and the loss of his family. At that age no matter how grown up a person is, they are not ready for that kind of responsibility, especially under those conditions. Jason grew up believing that anytime he would get close to someone they would surely leave. He said that he felt responsible for his family's death.

He had a challenging time forgiving his parents, especially his mother, for leaving him to fend for himself. Jason lived with his pain for 25 years. That is how long it took him to go to his mother's graveside and forgive her--work that would free him. One day he finally said; "This is what I need to do before I can get on with my life." Jason did get on with his life and he is one of the greatest people on this earth. He said that without working through his forgiveness process, he would still be drinking and taking drugs to ease his pain. Jason spent many years running from the fear of abandonment. It's been said fear is a thief that robs you of your future. Because of that fear, he was not able to forgive and accept the healing that needed to take place.

    You may have noticed that Jason moved into the forgiveness after his family was gone. You might ask how is that possible. How can you forgive someone when they are no longer here on this earth? Do you still hold images in your mind of people you either loved or just barely knew? Because someone leaves this earthly plane does not mean they do not exist. Their energy is very much alive and wants for you to move past any and all pain that keeps you locked up. Remember, energy can neither be destroyed nor created. The picture you hold of them enables you to find the freedom from all that keeps you bound. The key is in your heart. Go "there," ask for and give the forgiveness that is essential to your evolvement and growth.

    The people of our lives are not the only living things from whom we need to ask forgiveness, or in some cases, give forgiveness.

Have you ever hurt an animal? Has an animal ever hurt you? If the answer is yes to either one of these then you have forgiveness work to do with that animal.

By now some of you might be saying something like, animals don't have feelings. However, you do and you are the one who benefits from the art of forgiveness in all cases. The following stories helped to shift my awareness that animals do indeed have feelings.

As were many young "men" growing up, I too was given a rifle for a birthday gift and set out to be the hunter-to hang the trophy and fill the larder. As we trekked through the woods on my first and only hunting trip, I came across the only deer I ever shot. It was a doe. At first I was very excited since I had spotted one early in the day. I raised the rifle and fired the shot. What took place next ripped my heart out-the blood-curdling cry of that creature. The cry of that doe was so painful to me that all I wanted was to take that moment back. In the film <u>Powder</u> the main character grabs the wrist of the hunter and then places his own hand on the wounded animal to transfer the pain of the deer to the hunter. The hunter actually experiences the pain of the animal at a depth most of us can't even imagine-because it's *only* an animal. It was like that for me. I felt the pain of that deer though the cries. I did not know the full scope of asking forgiveness at that time in my life but I knew I had to ask.

Ironically I have a friend who has been a hunter for many years. He was shot a couple of years ago and survived. During his recovery I ask him if he now knows what the animal feels when the bullet strikes? He said yes and would never wish that on anyone. He stills goes hunting, but he has a whole new appreciation for life, and shoots with his camera. This is not judgment, pro or con, about hunting; it is a true story that took me to a deeper level of sensitivity.

I believe there is a part of all us that recognize an opportunity to make retribution to the people or things we may have hurt. It was a number of years after I had taken that doe's life that I was given the chance to "help" another life. As I was driving out of Portland, Oregon on Highway 84 East through the beautiful gorge, I noticed a yearling, a fawn, running down the middle of the highway the same direction I was traveling. The deer could not get off the road because he was too small and too tired to jump the roads concrete barriers. The other vehicles were slowing down to avoiding hitting him but did not attempt to stop. At the time I did not know what but something told me I had to help this creature. I drove past this little animal, stopped, got out of my car and positioned myself right in front of this young creature of God. It was amazing to me that all the traffic stopped when they saw what I was trying to do. I stood firm as this little, tired, scared animal moved closer. He tried to go around me but because he was so tired from running, he ran right into my arms. At that time I took this little creature and placed him over the barrier and watched him run off to safety. It was in the saving of this animal that my forgiveness was complete.

As I mentioned, I believe we are all given the opportunity to rectify the hurt we have caused all living things, not just people, and often it is for someone or something else. In the same way, don't we experience kindness from someone who "owes us nothing?"

Almost thirteen years ago I received a gift from the Universe in the form of two kittens. They are Norwegian Forest Cats. The greatest pets I have ever had the honor of taking care of. Their names are Abbott and Costello. At the time, I was living in a pretty nice home with my partner and love interest. We often worked in the yard to make it look nice. Like many people, we placed bark dust in the flowerbeds. On sunny days both cats loved to lounge around the house in the bark dust. Upon entering the house after work one day, I noticed what appeared to be a piece of bark dust hanging from Costello's ear. I naturally went over to him to pull the bark dust from his ear. As I attempted to pull that piece of bark dust off his ear he let out a meow(ch) like you hear when you step on a cat's tail. It was not bark dust; it was a piece of his ear.

Costello was a little fighter. He took it upon himself to be the guard dog of the house and keep other cats away. It was apparent to me he had been fighting. In the exchange the other cat had "mangled" Costello's ear and left a piece hanging.

After discovering it was a part of his ear hanging there, I called the vet to ask what it would cost to have it removed. They told me $100.00. I said no thanks; I'll do it myself. By this time my partner had arrived home. I asked her to be my nurse and hold him down so we could remove that part of his ear. I carefully took two cubes of ice and placed them over Costello's ear to numb it. After a few minutes I reached for his ear with the scissors. I have always known that animals have feelings, especially after the experience with the deer, but this is where I really became aware that animals *do* feel. As I went to clip that piece of ear off I looked at Costello's face only to notice tears running down his cheek. I said, "Forgive me, Buddy, this has to be done." He trusted me enough to be calm and allow me to do what needed to be done. In an instant it was over. Both my partner and I felt a tremendous amount of compassion toward this little animal. Since then, I have retraced all the animals I may have hurt and asked for forgiveness. I have also forgiven the ones that have hurt me.

How do you give and receive forgiveness? There are several ways to work with forgiveness and I encourage you to find the one that is most comfortable for you. The one I found best for me when I had a lot of forgiveness work to do is a process called recapitulation.

Recapitulation is a summary or synopsis built around those with whom you have unfinished work. The best way to initiate the process is to find a quiet place where you won't be disturbed and imagine a stage in front of you. Imagine moving across the stage, one by one, those you have determined you need to ask forgiveness from or those you need forgive. In some cases you may find yourself both giving and receiving forgiveness. As you bring each one to the center of the stage, have them stop and imagine that between you is a string of energy that connects the two of you. Start a dialog between the two of you. I really have no advice as to what you should say, since each one of you, as well as those you are about to work with will have different issues unresolved from the past.

I can tell you this; you will know what to say and the questions to ask when the time is right.

Some of this may be difficult at first, because of the emotions that will arise, especially if the wounds are deep. All emotions are welcomed and talked about. When emotional feelings arise you might find yourself wanting to back away; the pain might seem too intense. However, keep in mind that you have unlocked the door to that which may be holding you hostage, and it is the perfect time to examine it with that person and talk about what hurt you or the reasons you hurt them.

In the scope of time it could take only a few minutes to come to a perfect understanding with that person or it could take more than one session. If you have a large amount of pain and many issues as well as a lot of people to work with, I do not recommend you attempt doing it all at the same time. Do only what you can handle in each encounter. The more relationships you clear up, the deeper the desire to continue. Throughout the day you may find reminders of unhealed situations in your life-irritations, sadness, pushed buttons. Make a mental note of what surfaces and work with it as soon as possible. These reminders come to us as we heal all that needs to be healed. I also recommend you find a counselor of your choice if the pain and issues are too deep for you to work with on your own. Once again, if you are wondering *if* you have any forgiveness work to do, ask yourself these two questions: Am I breathing and do I have a heartbeat?

As understanding and forgiveness move between you and the ones you have chosen to work with, there will be a time to let them go. You accomplish this is by imagining you have a pair of scissors in your hand. Once you have agreed it is time for both of you to move on, bless them and wish them well, then, reach out and cut the energy cord you placed between you and them. Be assured you will feel a tremendous sense of lightness, freedom, compassion and Love.

As I mentioned earlier, when we forgive those who have hurt us, we do it not for them but for ourselves. Earlier I compared a lack of forgiveness to taking poison and expecting the other person to die. It bears repeating. The longer you hold onto those things that no longer serve you – resentment, hurt or anger -- the more you poison yourself, your own body. "How can that be, you might ask?"

There are documented cases of people whose health deteriorated because they were not willing to let go of their "thoughts" of unfairness that "happened" to them. The pain and hurt we feel may have been unfair, but continuing to poison ourselves is our choice. Confucius said, "Why let a man beat you twice? First he does a wrong thing to you, and then you make yourself miserable by hating him for it.

> A noted physician, talking before a group of other medical men on this very subject, was recorded as having said in his concluding remarks, 'Abnormal tumors and cancers are due to a long period of suppressed grief and anxiety.'

> This is another way of saying that such diseases are due to a lot of sinful thoughts getting bottled up and suppressed within our minds. Raymond Holliwell, <u>Working with The Law.</u>

The physical result of my obsession to "pay back" the woman that hurt me was a chronic ulcer. It wasn't until I understood that anger and did the forgiveness process necessary that I was able to heal the ulcer. I am happy to report, contrary to the diagnosis I received, the ulcer is completely healed. I assure you that forgiveness played a huge role in that healing. You must trust in your healing also.

Is there an area of your body you have not been able to reclaim due to old issues unexposed or unresolved? How do you know what to look for? I think the best place to begin is to locate information on energy centers or charts for the body and how each area corresponds. You can find these charts in bookstores. Many massage therapists will share with you what each part of the body deals with in terms of unresolved emotional issues.

I can tell you that what you are about to do in your life might not be the easiest work you have done. However, if you proceed into the work as if it is already done, in other words, move through it in faith, you will notice a shift in your life you will call a miracle.

When you move through all areas of life in faith, you will begin to notice the doors opening for you, seemingly before you even put your in key. And that, Dear Reader, brings us to the next chapter, The Keys to Faith.

    I find it rather amazing how spirit has moved in my life. At the time I wrote all of my poems, I had no idea of the synchronicity that was taking place. At that time I did not know I would be writing about forgiveness as a doorway into our desired lives. Hence, the following poem:

Open the Door

*Experiences we go through are not just that,
sometimes the experience leaves us
wondering where we are at.
We know we have been there when it is done,
do we truly know what just went on?*

*You made a choice for that experience
when you opened the door,
now that door is closed,
in front of you stands many more.*

*For you to move to a new plateau
you must have learned what was needed,
If you learned nothing the next door
you open will be the experience repeated.*

*Each door you go through is
an experience all its own,
but know through the door
you will never walk alone.*

*You may not understand what
your current experience is for,
Know that when the experience is done,
there will be many passages waiting,
ask your spirit to help choose and
then Open the Door.*

9-95

Here is your
Key to Forgiveness.

As mentioned, we often think that forgiving someone is telling him or her it was ok for the hurt they caused us. As you read, forgiveness is not about them, but about you and how you carry on in your life.

Forgiveness is not about forgiving any given act that someone perpetrated. It is about forgiving the perpetrator and knowing and understanding that we do not know what is going on at any given time in anyone's life. We do not know what any one person has gone through in their life. Does this give them reason to hurt or harm another? Absolutely not.

What it gives you and me is pause for us to call up our compassion towards another and look deeper at ourselves and ask the question: What would I do if I were in that persons shoes? If you knew for a moment that a woman who had lost her temper towards you to the point where she said horrible things had just lost her child, how would you respond?

Ask yourself some key questions.

How many times have I been angry with a loved one for nothing at all?
Has being angry with that person worked for you in getting the result you want?

Are you afraid to date because someone in a previous relationship treated you less than you would like to be treated? --OR-- Are you afraid to commit to someone nice because of what someone else did to you?

Have you hurt others in the past? Do you have some forgiveness to ask for so you can free yourself?

That essentially is what forgiveness is about. It is about releasing the hurt and pain so you can begin living a life of freedom. You forgive others not for them, but for yourself. You free yourself from the bondage of not feeling like you deserve to be loved or to be, do or have all the things you want in life.

With forgiveness comes freedom - freedom from the past. In that freedom you give yourself permission to start living in today, for today is the only place you can really live your life.

Doubt is hell in the human soul.

Catherine de Gasparin

Chapter Eight

The Keys to Faith

From the wisdom of the Universe, the wisdom of God, through me, only good pours forth into my world as a perfect manifestation.

From the wisdom of the Universe, the wisdom of God, through me, only good pours forth into my world as a perfect manifestation.

From the wisdom of the Universe, the wisdom of God, through me, only good pours forth into my world as a perfect manifestation.

From the wisdom of the Universe, the wisdom of God, through me, only good pours forth into my world as a perfect manifestation.

You may wonder why I repeated the same phrase over and over. The answer is simple. I want to know if you believe it. If not, why not? Which leads us to another question. Do you believe that the good in this world is meant for you as well as others? If you do not believe there is enough good in the world for you, then how can you believe you will receive all the good you desire? There is an abundance of good in this world and in this chapter we are going to look at how you can open yourself to all of it.

What you read above is a "positive affirmation" as mentioned in Chapter Two. If you do not believe that "only good pours forth" into *your* world, then you need to look at your belief system. As has been shown in earlier chapters, if you don't believe it first, then it will not happen. I know that might make some of you want to toss this book across the room, if you haven't already done so. Now that you have picked the book back up, please know that what I share with you, I share from experience. We have been conditioned "to see it is to believe it." I, like most of the population, was raised to believe the same. In other words, we have been conditioned that until we see it in front of us, we should not believe in its existence. Looking back over the years, that kind of believing has never worked for me. It wasn't until I shifted my thinking, my beliefs and my faith, that life really started to work for me.

> When you believe that the good you ask for or pray for *will* happen, you are showing Faith; Then, because of that faith and belief you will *see* "your life" starting to work for you. Dr. Wayne Dyer, <u>You'll See It When You Believe It</u>.

If you can't quite believe that, remember a time when the good you wanted showed up in your life. Remember a time when you were planning an event in your life such as a ski trip or a vacation to a destination you thought about for long time. You didn't just happen to get there without knowing and believing that you could. When you first thought about the trip or were ask if you wanted to go you had to see it first in you mind. As the picture of you embarking upon that adventure grew in your mind, you believed it would happen. You were not concerned whether or not the trip was going to take place -- you just knew it could.

That is faith. You thought about what you wanted, you believed you could have it or do it, and you had the faith and took the action necessary to make it happen. "God helps those who help themselves."

So my question to you is, if you have the faith and belief to accomplish what we might call everyday events and adventures, then what is it that stops you from having enough faith to realize the greater things in your life?

The current belief systems we use in our thinking and languages are what stop all of us. The deeper part of our beliefs and what keeps us stuck is what our current belief system allows us to see in our physical world. I mentioned in an earlier chapter that what we see with our physical eye is a memory in the brain. In other words, as we grow up we come to know what a table is or what a dog is and because we believe it we don't have to think about it. We see the object and it triggers a recall in our memory center or belief center. We have a difficult time when attempting to see our world different or better than we believe it really is. We tend to get caught up in, "this is the way my life is" because that's what we "see" or believe.

Affirmations are important in creating better pictures in the imagination of our minds. When we repeat the same statement over and over again, our unconsciousness mind and our imagination begin to "see" things differently. It is our imagination that can change our outer world. How, you ask, is that possible? Your unconscious mind does not know the difference between the real and imagined worlds.

If you think about something long enough, imagine its existence, then you will believe it is true, and it will manifest in your life, even if it is a lie.

I am going to give you a little exercise in the power imagination. Many of you may have tried the lemon exercise, where you imagine the bitterness of the lemon in your mouth and how real it can be. I would even venture that some of you taste the lemon as your mouth salivates while you are reading this.

That is not the exercise. This is: I want you to sit back in a quite place and relax.

Now, let your imagination begin to see yourself getting sick. Your temperature begins to rise. You notice yourself starting to get a little nauseated and you begin to get uncomfortable. The next thing you know, you're really sweaty and cold at the same time. You are beginning to feel too weak to get up, but you know you have to make that trip to the restroom because there is a chance you might have a moment where what is inside of you will make its debut as you hug the commode. You make the determination you need to call the doctor.

By this time you are telling me that I must be crazy to have you do such a process. You are saying, "Why in the world would I imagine myself getting sick?" You are right, why would you? Scratch that thought from your mind. You now see how your imagination can work at manifesting "anything" you want. If you believed strongly enough that you could make yourself sick, then why can you not believe that you can be, do and have all that you want in this life?

Now that I have your attention on how powerful your mind is when you believe in something strong enough, it is time to share with you how faith and belief work together.

It has been said that belief is the great activator of faith. When you have self-confidence to accomplish that which you set out to do, you believe in yourself; therefore, you have faith in who you are. Without that belief and the faith in who you are or what you are about to do, you would not do it. The big difference between belief and faith is that you can believe in almost anything. As mentioned above, if you believe that you can make yourself sick, you will. If you believe strongly enough that you can make yourself wealthy, you will take the actions to become wealthy. However, behind the belief you hold in your mind is the biggest difference between the two, the separation between Faith and belief. Faith is only for the good in your lives. Belief can be for the positive or the negative. You can believe in the negatives but you can only have faith in the good. You cannot use faith in drawing negatives to you. Consider all the times that you wanted something so delightful you just "knew" you would have it. Also consider "the bad things," as we label them, which have come into your life. At some level you believed that thing or event would occur. You probably had a certain amount of anxiety because you believed it so deeply, but you never held the faith that something bad would happen to you.

You might ask, if faith is so powerful then why would you need to believe in anything other than the faith itself? What is the purpose of belief?

"Faith without belief is like having a fortune and forgetting where you put it. When you believe your good can be drawn to you then your faith moves it into expression." <u>Twelve Gifts from God.</u> By William Warch

    It is in your undying faith that you can and will draw to you all that you desire. As mentioned earlier, you must first "see" that which you desire in your mind, and believe that it is already here or on its way. In that believing or knowing, that which you have asked for will show up in your life. When you know without any doubts, you are acting in faith.

    The best personal account I can give you in acting in faith is when I moved into my own condo within eight months of being homeless. I started practicing the principles written about throughout this book and put into deep practice acting as if, acting in faith that I would have my own place. Not only did I end up *buying* my condo I was able to fully furnish it with the nice furniture I had in storage and could not sell. I attempted to sell all my furniture at one time for money so I could eat. All I can say is that God knew I would need my furniture.

    There is another area in our lives where faith plays one of its most significant roles. That is the area known as tragedy. When something happens that threatens a loved one, or even those we read about in the news, we move into an autopilot mode about how bad that incident was. When we hear about someone getting raped, it is unpleasant and tragic and most of us would never wish that on anybody. However, if we move through that misfortune with faith that there is some greater good that will reveal itself in time, we can heal those wounds a little earlier. Please know that I am not suggesting you by-pass the grieving and healing process in any unfortunate circumstance that may take place in your life. I am only suggesting you include in your process the act of faith that the greater good will be shown to you.

The following story is an account of how faith can move through your life at a time of tragedy and heartbreak.

Two years ago in August a friend of mine lost her son when he drowned. Normally, I would ask you to imagine what she was feeling at a time like that. However, unless you have lost a child there is no amount of imagination that could make it real enough to know exactly what that parent is feeling. I have two close friends who have lost their children and I cannot even *begin* to imagine what they felt or are feeling.

It was a Saturday morning; my friend Ruth and her partner Howard invited me over for breakfast. We enjoyed each other's company as well as the meal, set in the German tradition. The phone rang. Howard left the table to answer it. He returned and told Ruth, it was her son, Jeff. She left to take the call. A little while later she returned to the table visibly emotional and shared with us that Jeff had called to share a birthday wish for the sibling he had lost. It was the birthday of Ruth's son, Nathan, who had made his transition from this world. As Ruth continued to share with the two of us her feelings of what the day represented, it became very clear that this day actually represented a new beginning in her life. In effect, it was a birthday for her; she released her personal struggles with her son's transition. In her endurance and holding onto the faith and belief that good exists in all things, she knew that good would surface. Clinging to her absolute faith she was able to move that mountain of grief.

Jesus said, "Have ye the faith of a mustard seed and say to the mountain, move, and the mountain will surely move." What does that mean? If you show the Universe that you have even a small amount of absolute, sincere faith, then the mountains in your own life will move beyond what you currently now think you can only do with strength. When you cling to even a small measure of faith, that of a mustard seed, you can move things in your life that strength alone cannot budge. It is in possessing true faith that you will gain the strength you need to accomplish anything you want. I say "true faith" since there is the smaller part known as blind faith. If we were to hold onto blind faith, which is an intuitive trust in that Spiritual Intelligence we've read about, you would surely, if you persisted, realize your dreams in time. Why wait?

Begin now by understanding faith. Bring faith to the forefront of your conscious mind. When you understand faith you know that you cannot have one thing in this world without having the converse that makes it complete-that balances. You cannot have the light without the dark. You cannot have the left without the right. You cannot have the top without the bottom. Try cutting a piece of fruit in half. You still have a left and a right. We often say, "Take the top off of "that." The top is not gone it has only changed shape. There is still a top and a bottom. You cannot have one without the other. So it is with you and me. You cannot have this life without having all the rewards that go along with it. It only takes a shift in your awareness and your thinking, as we discussed in chapter one, to begin to understand faith. As you begin to trust with faith, you will come to know that all of your experiences are for your greater good. When you know all the experiences you go through are for your highest good, you can and will move through your life with greater ease and grace.

    When the idea, or God thought, as I like to call it, came to write this book, I did not question if it could be done. I knew that not only could it be, but it also had to be, and I held strong to the faith that the words would be delivered to me. I actively believed it would be done by faithfully staying with it. Since this is my first book and I acted in faith, it has been easier than I thought it would be. Of course, when you're talking Truth, it is never hard.

> "Faith without works is dead!"
> James 2:17

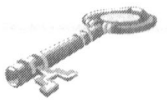

Here is your Key to Faith

As mentioned in the opening of this chapter we have been conditioned to see it is to believe it. I know in my own life that philosophy has not worked. Has it worked for you?

Here is a short story about faith. There was one particular week in my life as I was attempting to launch a new product into the auto industry that was reminiscent of Mother Hubbard's cupboards. I was literally down to one potato in my cupboard. The first thing I did was to give gratitude for that one potato for it meant I had something to eat. I had no visible money to buy any food with. The second thing I did was to go about my business acting as if all I needed was already here. I went through the day knowing that God would not let me down. I went to the mailbox later that day and found a check for $135.00 that I never expected. It was enough to carry me through until my next form of income showed up.

I had two choices. Either I could panic and worry about not having any food or I could show the Divine that I trusted I would be ok. I chose OK!

What is taking place in your life right now that might look like a situation that would constitute worry?

Are you worried or scared that you might not have enough food? As you know by now holding onto the fear only draws to you that which you fear.

Here's a question I would really like you to ponder. Have you ever *not* been taken care of? If you are answering yes then that answer is from a place of, I didn't get taken care of the way I wanted. In other words you had expectations about how the next thing or meal were to show up in your life.

What does faith look like? If I were to give it a description it would look like your whole world is operating in a total state of peace and tranquility. That state of peace comes from a state of absolute knowing that all is in Divine order and that which you are holding in your mind is for the highest and best for all concerned.

In Conclusion

As you work your way through the keys outlined in this book please be aware that your life will change and you will draw to you all that you ask. I strongly urge you to monitor your thoughts as well as your actions. Remember, if you are holding negative thoughts about yourself and the world around you, you will not move in the direction of your true heart's desire. You will draw to you the thoughts you harbor and dwell upon.

We have all heard that life is a puzzle. It is also true with spirituality. You must obtain the knowledge, the pieces of the puzzle, of each Spiritual Law, Gratitude, Faith, Love and so on before you can consummate your dreams. There is a piece of the Spiritual puzzle for each area of your life. You determine which area of the puzzle you need to work on first, and then move to the next one accordingly. As you work with each piece and understand how that law works in your life, you have unlocked that mystery. The pieces in this book are like that of the first puzzles you ever put together. They are only the beginning of a whole library of puzzles you will want to explore when you have completed this puzzle. As you get better at finding where each Law fits with the others in your life, you will want to move on to the bigger puzzles that will add to the knowledge you have gained here.

There is a suggested reading list at the back of this book that can assist you in revealing more of the greatness that is inherently inside of you.

When you first opened this book I was laying the pieces of the puzzle in front of you by giving you the keys to begin unlocking the mystery of each piece. As with any puzzle, you looked at the pieces and asked, "Where do I start?" As you lay out the pieces of your new puzzle, they may look something like this. Out of order.

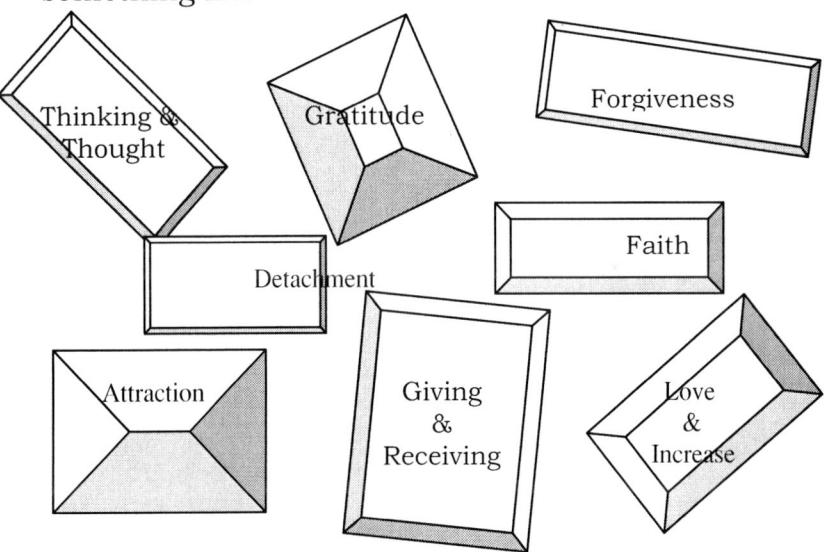

Take the time to study each piece. Study each Law and how they come together in your life. You will see where each connects with the other. When you find those connections between the pieces, the places in your life where the Laws fit together, you will find a connectedness within yourself that you may not have known existed. In recognizing that connectedness, it is highly possible you will feel at one with the whole universe, which of course you are.

As those pieces come together, notice order in the way they fit together. In noticing that order you will experience a sense of peace. When you began experiencing a sense of peace, the puzzle may look something like this.

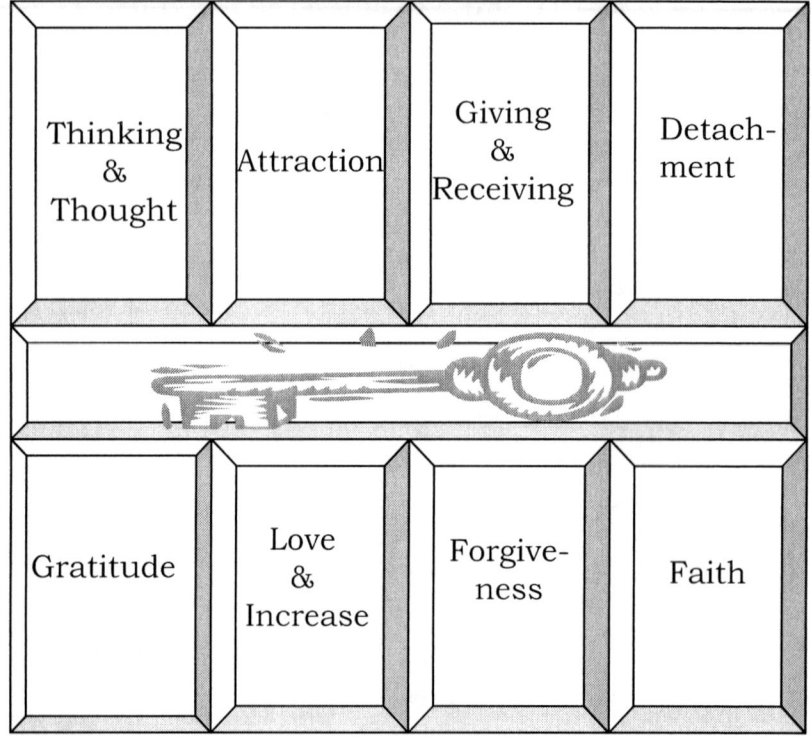

Your completed puzzle may look different than mine. The way you choose to unlock the mystery of each piece will determine how each piece; each spiritual law fits in your life. As you continue to unlock the mystery, and shape your puzzle, your life will unfold and be shaped in ways you never thought possible. Each of our lives will unfold according to the area we choose to work on. I would like to suggest the two most important keys to grab and areas to unlock first are those of forgiveness and gratitude.

The beauty of working with these Spiritual principles is that you can return to your puzzle and shift a piece, a Spiritual Law, to a place where the fit is more conducive to the growth you currently wish to experience or express. The order you choose will be right for you-what's important is that you work with these Laws, that you "use" the keys on a daily basis.

Most of us have seen the signs inside store windows that read:
"Help Wanted—Apply Within." There are times when our spirit or soul is holding a help wanted sign right in front of our face and we move past it because we don't see it or think the rewards won't be great enough. If we never stop and fill out the application, learning how to obtain the keys to the Spiritual Laws that truly govern our lives, we may never know how great the rewards can be. When we complete an application, we become aware of how the Divine works in our lives. Only then are the rewards to be received revealed to us. However, just filling in the blanks is not enough. As the sign said, "Apply Within." The greatest part about filling in the blanks is, you can never be rejected because you don't have the skills. Once you are finished filling in the blanks, you will be accepted immediately. Then all that is left to do is the inward application. The inward application of these Laws sets in motion the changes we have yearned for in our lives and we can't help but notice as these changes take place. Each time you bring to awareness another piece of the puzzle, unlock another mystery of how this Infinite Intelligence is here for each one of us; it is like completing another page of the application.

Now that you have learned what it takes to move toward fulfilling your dreams, in essence completing your application, it is now time to "Apply Within."

Thank you for taking the time to read, learn and understand what *you* can do to draw to you all that you desire. It has been a great pleasure to assist you in unlocking and uncovering some of the avenues I know will lead you closer to *all* your dreams and desires. It is in serving you, and bringing to you the knowledge that Jesus was sharing with us, the knowledge of how God *really* works in our lives, that I have encountered within myself a great deal of healing and received more abundance than I ever thought imaginable. I honor each one of you for taking the time to learn more about yourself and how these spiritual principles affect your life-whether working them or not. By sharing this ancient knowledge with you, my desires are manifesting now. I send you blessings and have faith that you too, will encounter the experience of manifesting your highest dreams and true abundance for your life.

The keys to your life are in your hands.

God Bless You!

I leave you with a poem written by a gentleman I met in Medford Oregon and a Prayer.

EMERGENCE

Would that I had the infinite wisdom,
To tell you what to do,
To plot your course to happiness,
With love and money too.

But alas, what wisdom's mine,
Is mine for me alone.
The only wisdom you can have,
Is the music and the tone,
You give your life this very day,
As you work and as you play.
With each success and each strife,
It's you who gives your life, its life.

<u>William J. Colson,</u> March 1979

This is my daily core prayer.

Good morning God. Thank you God for this day. I give gratitude for this day. I give gratitude for my breath and my life in this day. I give gratitude for the opportunity to be of service today.

I ask that you walk with me, talk with me, guide me, direct me, lead me where you would have me be of the highest service today God. I ask that you guide my thoughts, my words, my actions and my deeds that they are of the highest, most impeccable, honoring and supportive to all those I interact with this day, *including myself.*

I ask Lord that you pour blessings upon me today and that you guide me in knowing how to be a good steward to the blessings and gifts you bestow upon me.

I ask that you pour blessings upon all beings I interact with this day. Use me Lord as your channel to share with those the gifts and blessings you would have them open to receive. Use me God as the channel for the Love, Peace, Joy, Abundance and Prosperity you would want those I interact with to experience.

I then add any names of the loved ones and those that come to mind that may need a prayer and just to ask God to watch over them.

I give gratitude at the end of each day as well. I give gratitude for all the gifts and blessings God has bestowed upon me even if some of the things didn't or don't look like gifts. When I say gifts I am referring to *ALL* the "things" that happened throughout the day. There are some things that happen that could be considered less than perfect and not what we think should have happened. These too are gifts. We only need to look for the gift and the blessing within.

    When we give gratitude for all things especially those things that may be painful then we begin to release the potential hold it could have over us.

Your Journey Begins Here

I leave you with a few blank pages so that you may journal your thoughts, feelings and experiences as you begin unlocking the mystery. Please keep in mind that this journey is a process. Learn how to use these keys and the next time you come to an area that needs unlocking you will not have to fumble with the key ring trying to locate the key you need.

Your Journey Continues...

Your Journey Continues...

Your Journey Continues...

About the Author

As a boy growing up in a family of six kids, David was always the one to keep the dreams alive. He knew how to bring light and laughter to all those around him. David's happy go lucky attitude about life seemed to make the dark days brighter. David's strength comes from when his own father denied that he was his child, according to his mother. The greatness recognized in being essentially fatherless is that he did not have the outdated schooling that most young men grew up with. Without the, "Be a man" teachings, David entered the adult world as a man of compassion with his own denial and hurt. He cared and gave greatly to others never acknowledging his own worth.

In addition to the lack of recognition from David's father he grew up as many in our world did, under strict religious fears and the dogma that ignorance brings with it. At age fourteen David was so full confusion about who or what God is that he decided not attend church any further. Under the influence of that confusion he devised a plan to get out of church the following Sunday. Knowing his mother would never accept him saying he's not going to church he went out into the families back yard the Saturday before and proceeded to rub poison oak over much of his body. Since David lacked a more complete understanding of how God plays a role in all of our lives he was not aware that God had heard his cries to break away from that which essentially left him empty. As Sunday morning rolled around he not only woke up with poison oak but also woke up with the measles.

He spent the better part of a week in a cold soda bath just to keep his body cool. This is the day he became spiritually homeless.

As an adult he spent a period of time without a home. Now he was spiritually and physically homeless. It wasn't until he was living out of a garage that he hit bottom. One day he had only one potato left to eat. This was the day David embodied the spiritual principles he writes about. This was the day he came home spiritually.

Within eight months of putting the principles he writes about here into practice David moved into his own condo, fully furnished.

It wasn't until twenty years later when David returned to a spiritual path, that he realized that God had everything under control, *then and now.* Seven years later, twenty-seven years from the time he left church he, as many people do, had this yearning or calling to belong. With such a strong pull to be a part of something larger David found a spiritual home, or maybe it found him, which he is now member and volunteer for many of the church's functions.

Growing up in the northwest David became a logger at the age of nineteen. In the three years he spent working in the woods he had four near death experiences. The first one came when he was just nineteen when 2,000 pounds of steel came within six inches of crushing him.

In July of 1996 he was in a serious car accident when another car struck him in the drivers door. Although thankfully there were no serious injuries, David spent the next five months in a neck brace recovering.

A few years prior to the accident he began a spiritual quest. It was in his recovery from the accident where he began looking at the deeper side of spiritual life. In that recovery he learned how to receive and accept his worth, something that is foreign to many of us. He learned that we all have value and self-worth no matter what our upbringing.

David spent 20 plus years of his life in sales, marketing and training giving his time learning how to serve others. David now serves you with the timeless knowledge that is here for each one of us.

David's current educational goals are to complete his studies and obtain his doctorate in Metaphysics as well as his Ministerial license so that he may serve you at a greater level.

One of David's goals is to help as many homeless people help themselves through showing them how to come home spiritually. His plan to accomplish this is to give as many free books as he can to the "residents of the street." The way he plans to do this is through a sponsorship program that is already creating free books for these individuals.

If you are interested in becoming a sponsor and providing a free copy to someone on the street or in the shelters please contact David at the information below.

Infinite Insights Intuitive Coaching

Phone: 503-626-6789
Email: idside2@SpiritOne.com

PO Box 230056
Tigard, OR 97281

THE BEGINNING IS THE MOST IMPORTANT PART OF THE WORK.

PLATO

There are only three choices in life:
The Past
　　The Present
　　　　The Future

You decide in which to live.

Situations happened
Yesterday
Promises Happen
Tomorrow
Life happens
NOW!
　　David Sides

David is the founder of Infinite Insights. Infinite Insights is a coaching venue that focuses upon you and your life. If you would like to experience coaching please email David at the address below.

As a purchaser or recipient of this book you are awarded a free coaching session, or discussion period, whatever you choose to call it.

The following list of books are a compilation of the materials I have drawn from over the years that have led me to experience what has been extolled here. I strongly encourage you to pick up the titles that *you* feel will assist you on your journey.

Title	Author

Building Your Field of Dreams --------------------
Rev. Mary Manin Morrissey

Talks on Truth-----------------------Charles Fillmore

The Science of Getting Rich-----Wallace D. Wattles

Working With the Law------------Raymond Holliwell

You Were Born Rich--------------------- Bob Proctor

How to Use Your Twelve Gifts from God-----------
William Warch

The Seven Spiritual Laws of Success--------------
Dr. Deepak Chopra

The Wisdom of The Ages   /
Manifest Your Destiny   /   Dr. Wayne Dyer
Your Scared Self   /
You'll See It When You Believe It

A Return to Love------------------------------------
Marianne Williamson

A Course in Miracles-------------------------------
Helen Schucman & William Thetford

The Celestine Prophecy----------------------------
James Redfield

The Power of Now----------------------------------
Eckhart Tolle

Building Your Field of Dreams can be obtained by contacting The Living Enrichment Center @ **1-800-893-1000** or by logging onto **www.lecworld.org** or at your favorite bookstore.